W9-BBL-673

NETIA.

S. Felice
S. Catarina
I. Crosechie
S. Ioan Bat:
S. Georgio Magiore
S. Marco
Palazzo Duca
S. Francesco
La Celestia
S. Iacoby Mar.
S. Lag: d. Rhodo

VENICE

COMMENTS BY

Byron
Dickens
Dürer
George Eliot
Henry James
Long fellow
Ruskin
Shelley
Wordsworth
and others

MARTIN HÜRLIMANN

VENICE

with 130 pictures in monochrome
and 18 color plates

INTRODUCED AND EDITED BY J. E. MORPURGO

A STUDIO BOOK

THE VIKING PRESS · NEW YORK

PUBLISHED IN 1964 BY THE VIKING PRESS, INC.

625 MADISON AVENUE, NEW YORK, N.Y. 10022

LIBRARY OF CONGRESS CATALOG CARD NUMBER 64-20683

TEXT PRINTED IN SWITZERLAND BY BUCHDRUCKEREI WINTERTHUR AG, WINTERTHUR

MONOCHROME PLATES PRINTED BY IMAGO, ZURICH

COLOR PLATES PRINTED BY CONZETT & HUBER, ZURICH

CONTENTS

INTRODUCTION

Venice is a glorious hussy, somewhat overblown, perhaps, given to ostentation and to the use of heavy make-up, certainly past her prime but still undeniably alluring. She was always grasping. Even the bones of her patron saint she acquired by theft in Alexandria and had them shipped home in a barrel of pork in order to scare off the prying Muslim. If she were entitled to her aristocratic posturings then to this day the outstretched hand could well serve as her insignia. Instead she uses St Mark's winged lion and of that the most famous example in the whole of Venice is not Venetian at all but Viking lifted out of the port of Athens. Arrogance is part of the nature of Venice, but with it she permits herself a compensatory warmth towards those who forgive her weaknesses. Behind her confident front there was always pathos, uncertainty, even an incipient mental derangement and, in the last two centuries, pathos has turned into tragedy. Venice has lost her reason for existence, her riches, her energy. She has become a museum piece.

There the simile becomes fact. Venice is a fantastic museum in which even the guardians see themselves as items in the catalogue. And how the turnstiles click! The citizens of empires which supplanted the Venetian come back in their millions to gape, to admire and to sniff up with the sour, sweaty smell of the canals, the rich perfume of a half-Oriental past and of the romantic mythology created for the place for the most part not by the Venetians but by the predecessors of those very tourists whose pounds, dollars, marks and francs now keep Venice from sinking into the waters of bankruptcy.

The city has a rich imperial past, but in truth Venice was never one of the great and creative imperial powers. Most of the European empires of the Christian era have developed from small beginnings, worked up to a fine climax of power and then faded – not into insignificance, but into a comfortable middle-rank amongst the nations. Venice had her fabulous hour, when imperial exercise added huge riches to the huge richness which Venice had known since the tenth century. Thereafter Venice stuttered off into obscurity. The wondrous achievement of Venetian-Gothic was wrought in the century when Constantinople fell to the Turks, when Christopher Columbus discovered America and Vasco da Gama the route to India around the Cape of Good Hope. By the end of the fifteenth century History had turned its back upon a maritime people whose one geo-political advantage was easy access to the Mediterranean and the Levant.

In that century the Venetians had been conquerors. They had subdued vast areas of the Italian mainland and much beyond the seas so that still the remnants of their short excursion into empire are visible in the alien landscape of the Peloponnese, the Ionian and Aegean islands and Crete, but they had little to export, not men, not merchandise, not even a language which could achieve international currency. The Spaniards, the Portuguese and, in their early days as imperialists, the French tempered the covetousness which is an inevitable part of the inspiration for empire-building with the heartfelt certainty that, as fair exchange for the earthly riches wrung from them, they could take to the conquered peoples the possibility of eternal salvation. As much islanders as the British, the Venetians regarded their lagoons as a defence-system against the overweening influence of the Papacy. (Later Venice was the one great Italian city which came close to going the way of the Reformation.) The Spaniards, the Portuguese, the French and, more than any of these, the British and the Dutch offered themselves and their children to the establishment of new homelands in lands far away from home. Venice had available no surplus population for the tasks of colonization. The British exported certain notions of personal independence which in time developed into principles of common law and parliamentary democracy. The Dutch exported careful domesticity and commercial integrity. Happily for the rest of the world, the severe and aristocratic constitution which Venice suffered for almost a millennium was in the rest of the world beyond the intimacy of Venice incapable of adaptation and, as was demonstrated by Shakespeare (ever a better historian than he knew), commercial integrity was never a strong suit of the Venetians. The Venetians reached out, grabbed and brought back their fistfulls of gold to the Rialto. Riches and energy the Venetians spent on the aggrandizement of their tight-packed city.

Thus was the museum built and embellished with the works of such as Pisanello and Gentile da Fabriano, but–and this is part of the incipient pathos–Venice decadent is today almost more obvious than Venice triumphant. The Gothic and neo-Byzantine masterpieces are submerged in a mass established by Venetians who had lost the opportunities and the inspiration which comes with magnificence. In this sense (if not in the political or economic) decay was a slow process. To the city's medieval and Renaissance glories, the great and small churches and palaces, the architects of the sixteenth and seventeenth centuries–Palladio, Longhena, the Lombardis, Sansovino and Scamozzi–added their wild masterpieces, but many, indeed most of the palaces which line the canals are but indifferent examples of the late-seventeenth- and eighteenth-century styles. Elsewhere in Europe and even in colonial America the post-Renaissance builders coupled beauty and dignity with domestic comfort. Venice in her decline, like the Roman Empire to which in her origins she had been in so many ways the heir, settled for conspicuous luxury. The art of Venice, once a ringing tribute to distant triumph and local prosperity, turned introspective and nostalgic. Genius survived but Carlo Goldoni, that cheerful recorder of unimportance, the two Canalettos and Francesco Guardi were but journalists or archivists where their Venetians predecessors had been creators. The Sublime Republic, in the Middle Ages the most awesome power and the most peculiar political organization, continued pomp but without circumstance. By the time that Napoleon shrugged the Doge and his Council out of existence Venice was no longer the city of a dreaded oligarchy. Instead it had become the city of cicisbeism and of Giacomo Casanova.

Yet–and the thought is worth repetition and expansion–it was the eighteenth century which settled Venice, probably forever, in the visual and romantic memory of the rest of the world. It is not extraordinary that the Canalettos and Guardi painted such excellent likenesses of Venice; other and far lesser genius has done as much for places where the light is less helpful to the painter and the scene less dramatic. What seems extraordinary is that still in the 1960's Venice shows itself time and time again just like a Canaletto, that the departed tourist thinking back to his Venetian excursion, sponges from his mind the recollection of *vaporetti* or Harry's Bar and composes in

9

his memory another Guardi. It is not extraordinary that in the eighteenth century Venice became the one five-star and inevitable sight in the itinerary of the Grand Tour; it contained the most obvious and the most varied examples of those Gothic and Byzantine splendours which once more the rest of the world was learning to covet and to imitate. What seems extraordinary is that the inward recollection of Venice which has survived is not a memory of the riches, the rigidity and the oppression of the Doges, but the gaiety and irresponsibility of eighteenth-century Venetians. Venice, for all its still-visible demonstration of power and achievement, holds the sentiment of the world as the place for lovers, on whichever side of the blanket they may make love.

The seemingly extraordinary becomes more nearly explicable when one considers the unusual – indeed, the unique – nature of the city. It is a miracle that it exists, built as it has been from its origins in the Dark Ages on mud and water, and its internal commerce by way of the canals is to most of mankind, accustomed to the security of dry land, the greatest miracle of all. The miraculous is often the paradoxical, and it is the nature of Venice that it demonstrates a series of paradoxes.

The absence of motor traffic makes Venice the least noisy city in the world (certainly it is the only Italian city in which it is possible to sleep peacefully, and even Venetian youth proves itself not truly Italian by eschewing the Vespa). But Venetian noises are among its most memorable peculiarities. The esoteric voice-signals of the gondoliers, the brutal whirring of the horde of pigeons above St Mark's Square and the rush-hour clattering of shoes on the floating *vaporetto* stages are all sounds which once heard remain forever Venice in the mind's ear.

The typical Venetian view is two-dimensional. Close-built to the edge of the canals, Venice presents itself as a mad and yet lovely tracery of brick and marble patterns as a back-cloth to the water-ballet. Yet nowhere else in the world is there such a substantial apron-stage for a city's drama, such a magnificent entrance-way to a city's life as that provided to Venice by the Piazzetta and the Piazza – and the grandeur of the Doge's Palace and St Mark's is quintessentially three-dimensional.

There are more churches to the Venetian square mile than to any other square mile in the world. (There is more of almost anything here than anywhere else except perhaps in that other island-city, New York, and New York is remarkably poor where Venice is rich – in churches and bridges.) Among the many there are quite a few of such magnificence as would serve as cathedral in most of the world's great centres of population. Longhena's Santa Maria della Salute, for example, or Titian's burial place (the proud possessor of one of his poorer altar-paintings), Santa Maria Gloriosa dei Frari, or again, so much belonging to Venice although separated from it, Palladio's San Giorgio Maggiore. There is, of course, San Pietro di Castello which was in truth the cathedral before Napoleon, and there is, even more of course, the Basilica of St Mark. And among the many are some built in such execrable taste as to appear blasphemous even to a Hottentot or an Englishman. 'The two churches of San Moisè and Santa Maria Zobenigo', wrote Ruskin, 'are among the most re-markable in Venice for their manifestation of insolent atheism.' A less devout ob-server may well see in the lapses of taste in Venetian church architecture signs of that same vulgarity which is so often apparent in Venetian glass.

Yet despite the number of its churches and whether they be good or bad, both in history and in contemporary life Venice is a remarkably unreligious city. Its heroes were merchants, adventurers, politicians and artists, not saints, nor even prelates. Still today the church bells ringing out over Venice give it part of its character, but the bells seem to call museum opening-hours and not Compline or High Mass.

Venice is a city of waterways and yet of all cities the most stimulating to explo-ration on foot. Tiny streets that go by names which have no logic to the visitor who moves by the Italian phrase-book (*Calle* and *Lista* among them) lead to exotic little bridges or to that bridge of all bridges, the Rialto Bridge over the Grand Canal, and from view to view. For the pedestrian there is here an archway, there a small *palazzo*, a street of market-stalls and then suddenly a quiet square with a huge cathedral of a church, or looming at the end of the little canal the worldliness of a cruising ship. There is bustle but no danger; nothing more lethal than a child's bicycle or a railway porter's trolley to persuade the eye to care instead of curiosity.

Time and time again as one thinks of Venice similes drawn from the vocabulary of the theatre come to mind. It is not merely the two-dimensional back-cloth of which I have written, nor yet the strengthening of an effect reminiscent of the theatre which comes with the fact that all the actors in the Venetian drama – be they crowd, bit-player or lead, historical, mythological or contemporary – must quite literally *walk* on stage. (Wagner was one of these actors, so perhaps we should have been permitted an occasional entrance on a sturdy white horse!) There is more to it than this. Venice was always isolated; the characters come in, act out their Venetian lives and then either die on stage or else go back to the wings beyond the lagoon and beyond the seas. And even within Venice – a city with only one long vista, the Grand Canal – there is a plethora of small stages, each to this day presenting its own drama. A tiny basin in which the gondolas tie up and the gondoliers bully the tourist with invitations and demands which vary from the exorbitant only down to the not quite so exorbitant; the shuffling crowd-scenes along the Riva degli Schiavoni, up and down, down and up, like *Aida* performed on an economy budget; the grumbling and teasing of the market-stall holders in Erberia; the rare hustling on the steps of the modern railway station; the roar and sweep of the motor launches of the fire-brigade; all are one-act plays and all seemingly inconsequential.

Throughout their history the Venetians have recognized dramatic possibilities and improved upon them, making the play into a pageant. Once a year on Ascension Day aboard his golden galley the Doge at the head of a great procession of gondolas set out to the open sea beyond the Lido there to cast a ring into the water in celebration of the continuing marriage of the Serenissima and the sea. The words of the ceremony had all the grandeur of liturgical Latin: *Desponsamus te, Mare, in signum veri perpetuique domini*. 'We take thee in marriage, O Sea, in witness of true and perpetual dominion.' Once a year on the patronal day each Venetian husband gave to his wife a red rose, a symbol of constancy. The Doges, again like the Roman emperors whose function they imitated so closely, were forever organizing circuses in order to keep their subjects from dwelling too much upon bread or liberty. There was even a nicely histrionic touch in building a bridge between the Doge's Palace and the dungeons so that the condemned could have a last ceremonious view of the route to the open sea and freedom. Still the twentieth-century Venetian can make a spectacle out of a gondola-borne wedding-party and a pageant even more lush out of a funeral. It is not surprising that the Film Festival is the most successful of all the more recent innovations.

On the grander scale, too, Venetian history has been punctuated with stage directions.

It began in this manner. 'Scene: a deserted island. Enter a small group of fisher-men. Their leader speaks. "We have fled the Franks as our forefathers their forefathers, the Huns, the Vandals and the Goths. Here we will build our refuge. I, your doge, proclaim it".'

And so it continued. 'Enter the Doge, Enrico Dandolo. He explains how he will enrich his people by exploiting the near bancruptcy of the Crusaders. Exits to lead them against Constantinople.' 'Enter Messer Marco Polo. Exits for Central Asia.' There are conspirators, bloody fights, extravaganza. And then: 'Enter Napoleon Bonaparte. *Exeunt omnes*.' The curtain falls and the Epilogue begins. 'Enter a chorus of strangers. They sing a song of admiration and delight.'

Given such consistent theatricality, small-scale and large, and it is no wonder that the only major Venetian writer was a dramatist.

As the eighteenth century settled Venice unchanged and unchangeable on the world's memory, so did the nineteenth century set it to paper. Venice was the holiday centre of the Romantic Movement. And then came the tourists, but already long before the era of Thomas Cook the foreigner had come to Venice for business or for pleasure and had stayed usually to admire and sometimes to hate the place. Because the past of Venice is ever-present the list of foreign residents is drawn by local geo-graphy rather than by chronology. As one walks around the city one sees them: Byron thinking of *Don Juan* and Teresa Giuccioli; his friend and master, Shelley; John Evelyn, Thomas Coryate and Sir Henry Wotton, Goethe, Hans Andersen, Jean Coc-teau, Rilke, Petrarch, Dürer, George Eliot, Dante, Duse, Wagner, Disraeli, Henry James, Ruskin, Whistler, Philippe de Commynes, the Brownings, Baron Corvo, who thought to set himself up as a photographer selling fine photographs to tourists ('Only, I firmly abhor from the notion that one might "begin small". For success, one must begin as one means to continue.'), Stendhal, Longfellow, Charles Reade, George Sand, Mrs Humphrey Ward, D. H. Lawrence. So the list of entries in the visitor's book – and so many of them Anglo-Saxon names – goes on and presumably will go on until Venice settles beneath the mud from which she rose.

They came to Venice, stayed and many of them died here: Robert Browning, Corvo, Wagner, Diaghileff all followed the example of Bolingbroke's banished Duke of Norfolk who

'retir'd himself
To Italy; and there at Venice gave
His body to that pleasant country's earth
And his pure soul unto his captain Christ'.

So many of these visitors wrote their impressions of Venice (thus compensating for the lack of a substantial local literary *corpus*) that the city echoes not only reminiscence but also a dictionary of half-remembered quotations. Philippe de Commynes, arriving as French Ambassador in 1495, wrote of the Grand Canal as 'methinks, the most lovely street in the world'. Just over a century later Coryate claimed that in his *Crudities* he had 'more particularly described... that most glorious, renowned and Virgin Citie of Venice, the Queen of the Christian World, that Diamond set in the ring of the Adriatique gulfe... than it hath been ever done before in our English tongue'. His description has seldom been surpassed and is still viable – so little has Venice changed since his day. Foreign writer after foreign writer set down his Venice. With Venice as model Ruskin set about changing the architectural taste of Europe. Byron and Shelley used Venice for sermons in poetry on the text of liberty – the Devil used in the service of God! And if the visual memory of Venice is eighteenth century, its literary representation is nineteenth. Venice was the Mecca of the Romantics and Neo-Romantics.

Not only the writers came, but also the painters: Dürer, Turner, Manet, Monet, Renoir, Dufy and Kokoschka have all painted the Venetian scene.

There is another class of visitor from the past: the visitor who never existed except as the creation of a writer's imagination. Indeed, for those who are sensitive to literary suggestion the character out of fiction is in Venice even more accessible than the character out of history. Call out the roll-call of these substantial wraiths and in its number each man will find his own favourites. As for me, I lead off with Othello and go on to Shylock, to Miss Bordereau and to the Duke of Plaza-Toro, not one of them a Venetian by the stricter definition, the Moor, the Jew, the American and the Spaniard, all of them in a sense exiles and yet all four so much of Venice.

Othello comes first on my list because his story holds so much that is a parable for all Venetian history: adventure, brutality, intrigue, betrayal, the whisper of Oriental origins and, finally, tragedy. He is here, too, as representative of the long line of hired soldiers who served Venice so well, the fictional *alter ego* of that greatest of her *condottieri,* Bartolomeo Colleoni, whose statue in the Campo Santi Giovanni e Paolo is perhaps the finest of the world's equestrian statues.

Shylock comes next, symbol of the Venetian truth that 'the trade and profit of this State consisteth of all nations'. His lively descendants flourish still in Venice; seeing them and seeing in the eye of the imagination Shylock among them, Antonio seems but a pampered boy and Portia something of a prig.

There is a Miss Bordereau in many a crumbling *palazzo* and fly-blown *pensione,* fugitive to the Venetian island, settled until death in the life of Venice and yet holding an Anglo-Saxon past as the only real present even in this more exotic setting.

As for the Duke: he is here for good historical reason, because Spain's time of influence over Venice must have its record even in fiction. But more than that: he is here because Venice cannot keep a straight face forever, everything Venetian must have a touch of the frivolous. Venice is an immediate invitation to the delivery of aphorism and apostrophe, but few have surpassed the entrance-lines onto the Venetian stage of the Duke of Plaza-Toro: 'As a Castilian hidalgo of ninety-five quarterings, I regret that I am unable to pay my state visit on a horse. As a Castilian hidalgo of that description, I should have preferred to ride through the streets of Venice; but owing, I presume, to an unusually wet season, the streets are in such a condition that equestrian exercise is impracticable.' (It was an old joke long before Gilbert put it into the Duke's patrician mouth. Thomas Coryate wrote of an Englishman of his acquaintance who went around bragging that he had 'ridden through Venice in post…as gross and palpable a fiction as ever was coyned'. Much later the American humorist, Robert Benchley, abbreviated the jest into a cable: 'Streets full of water. Please advise'. But as the Duke says, if for different reason, 'no matter', a good joke is never out of fashion.)

Fiction and fact, the past and the present are all in Venice so inextricably intermingled as to add all into one conglomerate of association. 'What news on the Rialto?' And the answer: all news from all time and many circumstances, bandied around by men and women who themselves are representative of many ages, many nations and many poets' dreams.

The first two unities are of no account; the third, the unity of place, is everything. It has its own symbol, the gondola, and its own herald, the gondolier. For almost one thousand years gondolas have plied the waters of Venice (the earliest document: a licence granted by the Doge Vitale Falier in 1094). There are gondolas and gondoliers in the foreground of many a Venetian painting, even in Gentile Bellini's *Miracle of the Cross* and in others that represent events which took place far from Venice. For example, there would seem to be no rhyme and little reason for the gondolas in Carpaccio's *Story of Saint Ursula* and yet they are as right and as natural as the Dutch beer-drinkers in Breughel's *No Room at the Inn*. The gondola is the signature of the Venetian painter, even more, it is the mark of realism, the touch of homeliness which brings the stability of fact to the service of otherwise unbridled imagination. The gondola glides early into every visitor's account of Venice. Hear Coryate, for example:

'None of them are open above, but fairly covered, first with some fifteene or sixteene little round peeces of timber that reach from one end to the other, and make a pretty kind of arch or vault in the Gondola…The ends are beautified with two pretty and ingenious devices in the forme of a Dolphin's tayle…The Watermen that row these never sit as our's do in London, but alwaies stand, and that at the farther end of the Gondola…and in my opinion they are altogether as swift as our rowers about London.'

(With this last opinion John Evelyn could not agree, saying that they are 'not comparable for swiftness to our common wherries'.)

Early in *The Aspern Papers* Miss Bordereau demonstrates her removal from her temporal and physical surroundings by remarking that 'it's many years since I have been in one of the gondolas'. In *Othello* the note of doom is first struck when Roderigo says to Brabantio:

'If't be your pleasure and most wise consent,
As partly I find it is, that your fair daughter,
At this odd-even and dull watch o'the night,
Transported with no worse nor better guard
But with a knave of common hire, a gondolier,
To the gross clasps of a lascivious Moor.'

16

(Indeed if there be lack of verisimilitude in *The Merchant of Venice* and also evidence for the inconceivable but generally-held view that Shakespeare was never in Italy, it stems from the fact that there are no gondolas for Shylock or Antonio, for Portia, the Prince of Aragon or the 'Magnificoes of Venice.')

But the gondola is not merely the centre piece of the mental picture of Venice, it carries also the agent by which that picture is created. Roderigo hinted at it and gave the hint sinister overtones, Gilbert's Marco and Giuseppe (literary lightweights alongside Roderigo, but nonetheless Venetians) proclaimed it openly – and amiably:

'We're called *gondolieri*
But that's a vagary
It's quite honorary
  The trade that we ply
For gallantry noted
Since we were short-coated,
To beauty devoted,
  Giuseppe and I.'

As he has been throughout the history of his trade, the gondolier is at once lover and conductor and messenger of love, he is the reincarnation of Casanova and also Casanova's boatman. Look closely at the modern gondolier (or investigate with care his predecessors) and the romantic notion shrinks. Listen to his vociferous and exorbitant demands and romance should evaporate. But some traditions are more powerful than logic. Other cities, Stockholm, Amsterdam and Rangoon among them, have their waterways. Florence has finer pictures, Rome, London and Paris have more substantial history. There are many cities, and in truth many small towns and tiny villages with buildings as fine as any in Venice. But Venice has something that all these others can offer and Venice has what they have not: gondolas and gondoliers.

Time's peaceful sequence has been shattered by the nasty roar of the *motoscafi*, those upstart motorized taxis whose owner drivers charge even more than gondoliers. Most Venetians and indeed most sensible tourists get from place to place by *vaporetto* and use gondolas only for short, almost ignominious fixed-price ferry-services. Gondolas must mix with coal-barges, with police-launches, with tired outboards, they must themselves be set (as indeed they always have been) to the task of transporting fruit and fish and the refuse of the city. They touch full glory only for an occasional *festa,* for the inevitable once-and-for-all-time gondola-trip of the foreign visitor to Venice, for weddings and, most glorious of all glories, for funerals. Yet the gondola is romantic Venice and will remain the symbol of Venice until the Grand Canal runs dry.

Out beyond the magic of the canals, the tiny streets, the lovely bridges, a long way from St Mark's and the Rialto, there is a world which is not Venice. It is linked to Venice by three thousand yards of railway and road bridge. Seeing these bridges in some other place one would be impressed by their magnificence, by the engineering skill of the Austrians who, as long ago as 1846, brought the railway into Venice, and of their Italian successors, who, almost a century later, made a way in (or almost in, for the road ends at the Piazzale Roma) for cars, coaches and lorries. But these two bridges come close to being the last line of a history-book. The island is an island no more, the city of water has been grabbed into the land mass. So it may seem, and so it seemed to those ardently insular Venetians who opposed both railway and road, their arguments deliciously reminiscent of British prejudice against the Channel Tunnel. Yet the reality is less clear. Certainly the bridges have deprived Venice of independence and inviolability. But the spirit of Venice wins: some insular magic reaches on to the bridges and turns incoming cars into galleys and railway-trains into 'argosies with portly sail'. Venice remains different and the difference is emphasized by the vagueness of the sea-scape on either side of the Causeways, a blank space on a page separating idea from idea.

Venice is still an island, set down in the waters of its own history, its own art, its own mythology, its own quick and lovable drama. There is much here for cynicism and much too for sly comment, and yet when all is said the finale is a paean to excitement, to beauty – and to the Venetians.

From the central stage in St Mark's Square Martin Hürlimann moves into the tiny back canals. He records generality and detail, sculpture, architecture – and urgent humanity. Through the medium of his camera he pins to the page a thousand years and today. Here is the quintessence of connected history and present excitement which is the mind's picture of Venice.

J. E. MORPURGO

18

2 Piazzetta

3 Piazza S. Marco

4 Vista dal Campanile di S. Giorgio Maggiore

5 Piazzetta

OCEAN'S NURSLING

Underneath day's azure eyes
Ocean's nursling, Venice lies,
A peopled labyrinth of walls,
Amphitrite's destined halls,
Which her hoary sire now paves
With his blue and beaming waves.
Lo! the sun upsprings behind,
Broad, red, radiant, half reclined
On the level quivering line
Of the waters crystalline;
And before that chasm of light,
As within a furnace bright
Column, tower, and dome, and spire
Shine like obelisks of fire,
Pointing with inconstant motion
From the altar of dark ocean
To the sapphire-tinted skies;
As the flames of sacrifice
From the marble shines did rise,
As to pierce the dome of gold
Where Apollo spoke of old.

Sun-girt City, thou has been
Ocean's child, and then his queen:

Now is come a darker day,
And thou soon must be his prey,
If the power that raised thee here
Hallow so thy watery bier
A less drear ruin then than now,
With thy conquest-branded brow
Stooping to the slave of slaves
From thy throne, among the waves
Wilt thou be, when the sea-mew
Flies, as once before it flew,
O'er thine isles depopulate,
And all is in its ancient state,
Save where many a palace gate,
With green sea-flowers overgrown
Like a rock of ocean's own,
Topples o'er the abandoned sea
As the tides change sullenly.
The fisher on his watery way,
Wandering at the close of day,
Will spread his sail and seize his car
Till he pass the gloomy shore,
Lest thy dead should, from their sleep
Bursting o'er the starlight deep,
Lead a rapid masque of death
O'er the waters of his path...

PERCY BYSSHE SHELLEY Lines Written Among the Euganean Hills, 1818

25

St Mark's

Darkness and mystery; confused recesses of building; artificial light employed in small quantity, but maintained with a constancy which seems to give it a kind of sacredness; preciousness of material easily comprehended by the vulgar eye; close air loaded with a sweet and peculiar odour associated only with religious services, solemn music, and tangible idols or images having popular legends attached to them; these, the stage properties of superstition, which have been from the beginning of the world, and must be to the end of it, employed by all nations, to produce a false awe in minds incapable of apprehending the true nature of the Deity, are assembled in St Mark's to a degree as far as I know unexampled in any other European church.

JOHN RUSKIN The Stones of Venice, 1851–53

One of the most beautiful churches in Western Europe

Like the Romans, the Venetians in the Middle Ages appear to have regarded the practice of the fine arts with indifference; they desired to emphasise the beauty of their city by architectural magnificence; they thought it proper to recognise the religion of the state by adding the lustre of mosaic and sculpture to its ceremonial; but it was sufficient to employ foreigners from Constantinople or Verona, or wherever else it might be, to do the work. There was, therefore, no native school of Venetian painting or sculpture to compare with those of Siena and Florence in the fourteenth century.

It is true that S. Marco was at that time one of the most beautiful churches in Western Europe; no mediaeval scheme of mosaics could compare with the twelfth and thirteenth century work in Venice; nowhere south of the Alps had the imagination of the sculptor formed such beautiful things, but so far as we know the character of everything depended upon the genius of men who were not Venetians. The ascetic and transcendental quality in mediaeval art was repugnant to a trading and pleasure-loving community whose habit was positive rather than speculative.

GRANT ALLEN Venice, 1898

6 S. Marco, Prima arcata   7 S. Marco, Facciata

The jewel-casket of the world

Venice recognized itself from the first as a strange and mysterious creation – the fruits of a higher power than human ingenuity. The solemn foundation of the city was the subject of a legend. On 25 March, 413, at midday the emigrants from Padua laid the first stone at the Rialto, that they might have a sacred, inviolable asylum amid the devastations of the barbarians. Later writers attributed to the founders the presentiment of the future greatness of the city; M. Antonio Sabellico, who has celebrated the event in the dignified flow of his hexameters, makes the priest, who completes the act of consecration, cry to heaven: 'When we hereafter attempt great things, grant us prosperity! Now we kneel before a poor altar, but if our vows are not made in vain, a hundred temples, O God, of gold and marble shall arise to Thee.' The Island city at the end of the fifteenth century was the jewel-casket of the world. It is so described by the same Sabellico, with its ancient cupolas, its leaning towers, its inlaid marble façades, its compressed splendour, where the richest decoration did not hinder the practical employment of every corner of space. He takes us to the crowded Piazza before San Giacometto at the Rialto, where the business of the world is transacted, not amid shouting and confusion, but with the subdued hum of many voices; where in the porticoes round the square and in those of the adjoining streets sit hundreds of moneychangers and goldsmiths, with endless rows of shops and warehouses above their heads. He describes the great Fondaco of the Germans beyond the bridge, where their goods and their dwellings lay, and before which their ships are drawn up side by side in the canal; higher up is a whole fleet laden with wine and oil, and parallel with it, on the shore swarming with porters, are the vaults of the merchants; then from the Rialto to the square of St Mark come

31

the inns and the perfumers' cabinets. So he conducts the reader from one quarter of the city to another till he comes at last to the two hospitals which were among those institutions of public utility nowhere so numerous as at Venice. Care for the people, in peace as well as in war, was characteristic of this Government, and its attention to the wounded, even to those of the enemy, excited the admiration of other States.

Public institutions of every kind found in Venice their pattern; the pensioning of retired servants was carried out systematically, and included a provision for widows and orphans. Wealth, political security and acquaintance with other countries, had matured the understanding of such questions. These slender fair-haired men, with quiet cautious steps, and deliberate speech, differed but slightly in costume and bearing from one another; ornaments, especially pearls were reserved for the women and girls. At that time the general prosperity, notwithstanding the losses sustained from the Turks, was still dazzling; the stores of energy which the city possessed and the prejudice in its favour diffused throughout Europe, enabled it at a much later time to survive the heavy blows which were inflicted by the discovery of the sea route to the Indies, by the fall of the Mamelukes in Egypt, and by the war of the League of Cambrai.

Jacob Burckhardt The Civilization of the Renaissance in Italy, 1860

S. Marco

10 Facciata

11 Porta maggiore

12 Mosaico dell'Atrio

S. Marco

15 Interno

16 Mosaico

17
Pala
Duc
Port
della
Cart

A great enchantress

Venice has long borne in the imagination of the world a distinctive position, something of the character of a great enchantress, a magician of the seas. Her growth between the water and the sky; her great palaces, solid and splendid, built, so to speak, on nothing; the wonderful glory of light and reflection about her; the glimmer of incessant brightness and movement; the absence of all those harsh, artificial sounds which vex the air in other towns, but which in her are replaced by harmonies of human voices, and by the liquid tinkle of the waves – all these unusual characteristics combine to make her a wonder and a prodigy. While there are scarcely any who are unmoved by her special charm, there are some who are entirely subdued by it, to whom the sight of her is a continual enchantment, and who never get beyond the sense of something miraculous, the rapture of the first vision. Not only does she 'shine where she stands', which even the poorest cluster of human habitations will do in the light of love: but all those walls, with the mist of ages like a bloom of eternal youth upon them – all those delicate pinnacles and carven stones, the arches and the pillars and the balconies, the fretted outlines that strike against the sky – shine too as with a light within that radiates into the clear sea-air; and every ripple on the great water-way, and every wave on the lagoon, and each little rivulet of a canal, like a line of light between the piles of masonry, which are themselves built of pearl and tints of ocean shells, shines too with an ever-varied, fantastic, enchanting glimmer of responsive brightness. In the light of summer mornings, in the glow of winter sunsets, Venice stands out upon the blue background, the sea that brims upwards to her very doors, the sky that sweeps in widening circles all around, radiant with an answering tone of light. She is all wonder, enchantment, the brightness and the glory of a dream. Her own children cannot enough paint her, praise her, celebrate her splendours: and to outdo if possible that patriotic enthusiasm has been the effort of many a stranger from afar.

Mrs Oliphant The Makers of Venice, 1899

Palaces of marble and porphyry

Venice was precisely fitted for the part her painters had to play. Free, isolated, wealthy, powerful; famous throughout Europe for the pomp of her state equipage, and for the immorality of her private manners; ruled by a prudent aristocracy, who spent vast wealth on public shows and on the maintenance of a more than imperial civic majesty: Venice, with her pavement of liquid chrysoprase, with her palaces of porphyry and marble, her frescoed façades, her quays and squares aglow with the costumes of the Levant, her lagoons afloat with the galleys of all nations, her churches floored with mosaics, her silvery domes and ceilings glittering with sculpture bathed in molten gold: Venice luxurious in the light and colour of a vaporous atmosphere, where sea-mists rose into the mounded summer clouds: arched over by the broad expanse of sky, bounded only by the horizon of waves and plain and distant mountain ranges and reflected in all its many hues of sunrise and sunset upon the glassy surface of smooth waters: Venice asleep like a miracle of opal or of pearl upon the bosom of an undulating lake: — here and here only on the face of the whole globe was the unique city wherein the pride of life might combine with the lustre of the physical universe to create and stimulate in the artist a sense of all that was most sumptuous in the pageant of the world of sense.

J. A. SYMONDS History of the Renaissance in Italy, 1875–86

18

Palazzo Ducale

19 Facciata meridionale

20 Vista generale

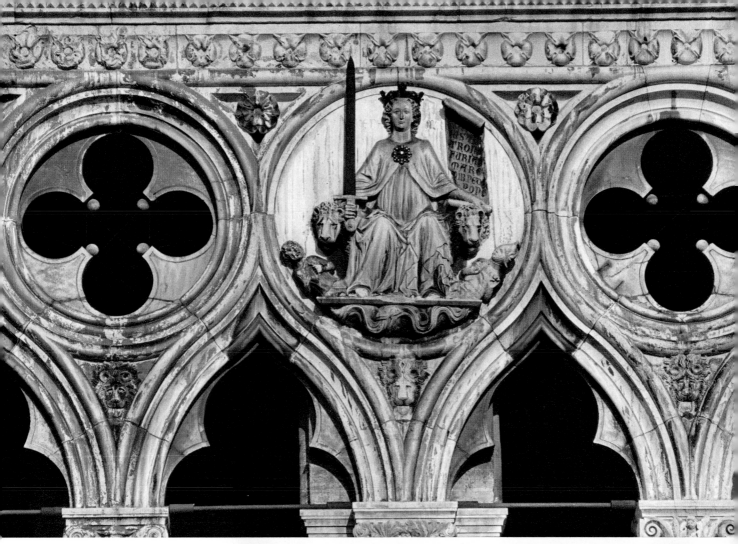

21 Facciata occidentale
22 Capitello

23, 24 Palazzo Ducale, Capitelli

Palazzo Ducale

25, 26 Ebbrezza di Noè

27 Eva

The Doge

The Adriatiq Sea, which they yearly espouse by casting a gold ring into it with greate pomp and ceremony on Ascension day...

The Doge, having heard masse in his robes of state (which are very particular, after the Eastern fashion), together with the Senat in their gownes, imbark'd in their gloriously painted, carved and gilded Bucentora, inviron'd and follow'd by innumerable gallys, gondolas, and boates, filled with spectators, some dressed in masquerade, trumpets, musiq, and canons; having rowed about a league into the Gulph, the Duke at the prow casts a gold ring and cup into the Sea, at which a loud acclamation is ecchoed from the greate guns of the Arsenal and at the Liddo.

Hence I pass'd thro' the Merceria, which is one of the most delicious streetes in the world for the sweetnesse of it, and is all the way on both sides tapistred as it were with cloth of gold, rich damasks and other silks, which the shops expose and hang before their houses from the first floore... to this add the perfumes, apothecaries shops, and the innumerable cages of nightingales which they keepe, that entertaine you with their melody from shop to shop, so that shutting your eyes you would imagine yourselfe in the country, when indeede you are in the middle of the Sea.

1646. In January Sign. Molino was chosen Doge of Venice, but the extreame snow that fell, and the cold, hindered my going to see the solemnity, so as I stirred not from Padoa till Shrovetide, when all the world repaire to Venice to see the folly and madnesse of the Carnevall; the women, men, and persons of all conditions disguising themselves in antiq dresses, with extravagant musiq and a thousand gambols, traversing the streetes from house to house, all places being then accessible and free to enter. Abroad, they fling eggs fill'd with sweete water, but sometimes not over sweete. They also have a barbarous costome of hunting bulls about the streetes and piazzas, which is very dangerous, the passages being generally narrow.

JOHN EVELYN Diary, 1641–1706

A market place of the world

The fairest place of all the citie (which is indeed of that admirable and incomparable beauty, that I thinke no place whatsoever eyther in Christendome or Paganisme may compare with it) is the Piazza, that is, the Market place of St Marke, or (as our English merchants commorant in Venice, doe call it) the place of S. Marke, in Latin Forum, or Platea Di Marci. Truely such is the stupendious (to use a strange Epitheton for so strange and rare a place as this) glory of it, that at my first entrance thereof it did even amaze or rather ravish my senses. For here is the greatest magnificence of architecture to be seene, that any place under the sunne doth yeelde. Here you may both see all manner of fashions of attire, and heare all the languages of Christendome, besides those that are spoken by the barbarous Ethnickes; the frequencie of people being so great twise a day, betwixt six of the clocke in the morning and eleven, and again betwixt fife in the afternoon and eight, that (as an elegant writer saith of it) a man may very properly call it rather Orbis then Urbis forum, that is, a market place of the world, not of the citie.

THOMAS CORYATE Coryat's Crudities, 1611

5
Torre dell'
Orologio

Superficial pastimes

The way to enjoy Venice is to follow the example of these people and make the most of simple pleasures. Almost all the pleasures of the place are simple; this may be maintained even under the imputation of ingenious paradox. There is no simpler pleasure than looking at a fine Titian – unless it be looking at a fine Tintoret, or strolling into St Mark's – it is abominable, the way one falls into the habit – and resting one's light-wearied eyes upon the windowless gloom; or than floating in a gondola, or hanging over a balcony, or taking one's coffee at Florian's. It is of these superficial pastimes that a Venetian day is composed, and the pleasure of the matter is in the emotions to which they minister. These, fortunately, are of the finest; otherwise, Venice would be insufferably dull. Reading Ruskin is good; reading the old records is, perhaps, better; but the best thing of all is simply staying on. The only way to care for Venice as she deserves it, is to give her a chance to touch you often – to linger and remain and return.

HENRY JAMES Portraits of Places, 1883

A SEA CYBELE

I stood in Venice, on the Bridge of Sighs,
A Palace and a prison on each hand;
I saw from out the wave her structures rise
As from the stroke of the Enchanter's wand:
A thousand Years their cloudy wings expand
Around me, and a dying Glory smiles
O'er the far times, when many a subject land
Looked to the winged Lion's marble piles,
Where Venice sate in state, throned on her hundred isles!

She looks a sea Cybele, fresh from Ocean,
Rising with her tiara of proud towers
At airy distance, with majestic motion,
A Ruler of the waters and their powers:
And such she was; – her daughters had their dowers
From spoils of nations, and the exhaustless East
Poured in her lap all gems in sparkling showers.
In purple was she robed, and of her feast
Monarchs partook, and deemed their dignity increased.

In Venice Tasso's echoes are no more,
And silent rows the songless Gondolier:
Her palaces are crumbling to the shore,
And Music meets not always now the ear:
Those days are gone – but Beauty is still here.
States fall – Arts fade – but Nature doth not die,
Nor yet forget how Venice once was dear,
The pleasant place of all festivity,
The Revel of the Earth – the Masque of Italy!

But unto us she hath a spell beyond
Her name in story, and her long array
Of mighty shadows, whose dim forms despond
Above the Dogeless city's vanished sway;
Ours is a trophy which will not decay
With the Rialto; Shylock and the Moor,
And Pierre, can not be swept or worn away –
The keystones of the Arch! though all were o'er
For us repeopled were the solitary shore...

I loved her from my boyhood – she to me
Was as a fairy city of the heart
Rising like water-columns from the sea –
Of Joy the sojourn, and of Wealth the mart;
And Otway, Radcliffe, Schiller, Shakespeare's art,
Had stamped her image in me, and even so,
Although I found her thus, we did not part;
Perchance even dearer in her day of woe
Than when she was a boast, a marvel, and a show.

LORD BYRON Childe Harold's Pilgrimage, 1812–18

67

Unique among the cities

The Venetian allure is partly a matter of movement. Venice has lost her silken dreamy spell, but her motion is still soothing and seductive. She is still a dappled city, tremulous and flickering, where the sunlight shimmers gently beneath the bridges, and the shadows shift slowly along the promenades.

And in the final analysis, the glory of the place lies in the grand fact of Venice herself: the brilliance and strangeness of her history, the wide melancholy lagoon that surrounds her, the convoluted sea-splendour that keeps her, to this day, unique among the cities.

JAMES MORRIS Venice, 1960

Streets paved with water

Venice is a wonderfully fine city. The approach to it over the laguna, with its domes and turrets glittering in a long line over the blue waves, is one of the finest architectural delusions in the world. It seems to have – and literally it has – its foundations in the sea. The silent streets are paved with water, and you hear nothing but the dashing of the oars, and the occasional cries of the gondolieri. I heard nothing of Tasso. The gondolas themselves are things of a most romantic and picturesque appearance; I can only compare them to moths of which a coffin might have been the chrysalis. They are hung with black, and painted black, and carpeted with grey; they curl at the prow and stern, and at the former there is a nondescript beak of shining steel, which glitters at the end of its long black mass.

PERCY BYSSHE SHELLEY to Thomas Love Peacock, 8 October 1818

43 S. Giorgio Maggiore, Interno

44 Ponte della Veneta marina

Riva degli
Schiavoni

Fondamenta
S. Biagio e
S. Maria
della Salute

Palazzo
Dandolo

48
S. Mois

Grotesque baroque

The gondola skirts Santa Chiara and the side of the Campo S. Marziale. The stretches of water become wider and speckled ripples roll slowly beneath the breeze with a quite indescribable mixture of blurred and fading shades. This is no ordinary water here. Enclosed within the canals, muddied by the ooze and seepage from the human colony, it has taken on an earthy redness, tints of pallid ochre, bluish and slimy dark patches, so that it resembles the accumulations of twenty different colours mixed together on the same palette. Under a northern sky it would be lugubrious; beneath the rays of the sun and the gentle azure silk which here drapes the entire cupola of heaven, it fills the eyes with an almost physical pleasure. Truly, one swims in light. The sky pours it down, the water colours it, the reflections multiply it a hundred-fold; as far as the white and pink houses everything throws the light back, and the poetry of shapes and forms completes the poetry of the day. Even in this wretched and abandoned quarter one sees palaces, façades decorated with columns. Indifferent or poor houses have large balconies enclosed with balustrades, windows scalloped with trefoils or capped with ogives, and reliefs of interlaced foliage and thorns. Dreams overcome one irresistibly. In vain does the canal of the Giudecca, almost empty now, seem to await the arrival of fleets to fill its noble port: one can think only of colours and lines. Three lines and three colours make up the entire scene: the wide moving glass, dark green, which shimmers with a harsh shining colour; above, standing out in sharp relief, the line of masonry which follows its curve; higher still, the clear, boundless, almost pale sky.

The boatman lands and insists that one should see the Church of the Gesuati. One perceives a pompous façade of gigantic composite columns, then a nave whose corinthian colonnade is set pretentiously in great pillars; at the sides, small chapels whose Greek façades bear curved corbels; a facing of mottled marble, an infinite number of insipid and thoroughly appropriate statues and bas-reliefs; on the ceiling, a pretty painting for a boudoir with fine pink and naked legs – in short, cold luxury, a show of costly affectation. The Italian eighteenth century is even worse than our own. Our works of art always retain a certain proportion because they retain a certain delicacy; as to them, they sit triumphantly among extravagance. Yesterday I saw a similar church, that of the Gesuiti. On the walls and parvis, green and white marble are inlaid to form flowers and floral designs. On the vaults, twisted gold delineates vases, pompons and flourishes, and the whole thing looks like the wall-paper for a drawing-room, all velvet and gold, whose price would tempt a parvenu. It is impossible to count the urns, lyres, streamers, foliage and white garlands which emboss the domes. Twisted columns of green marble with flakes of white support the canopy over the altar, where lean and sentimental statues – Christ with his cross, God the Father seated on an enormous globe of white marble – are displayed, borne up by angels; the pair take shelter under a roof of scaly marble, so baroque that one cannot help laughing. This grotesque over-emphasis bursts out even in the grand architectural lines; they are not content with ordinary forms, they have enlarged the vault of their nave so as to give it a low arch like that of a bridge, and they have flanked it with cupolas which resemble the hollow of a shield. One senses the effort of the imagination working in the void, resulting in a rhetoric of superlatives and conceits and contriving, in resounding and polished phrases, a form of drawing-room worship for ladies and for men of the world.

HIPPOLYTE TAINE Voyage en Italie, 1866

San Giorgio Maggiore

Straight across, before my windows, rose the great pink mass of San Giorgio Maggiore, which, for an ugly Palladian church, has a success beyond all reason. It is a success of position, of colour, of the immense detached Campanile, tipped with a tall gold angel. I know not whether it is because San Giorgio is so grandly conspicuous, and because it has a great deal of worn, faded-looking brickwork; but for many persons the whole place has a kind of suffusion of rosiness. If we were asked what is the leading colour at Venice we should say pink, and yet, after all, we cannot remember that this elegant tint occurs very often. It is a faint, shimmering, airy, watery pink; the bright sea-light seems to flush with it, and the pale whitish-green of lagoon and canal to drink it in. There is, indeed, in Venice a great deal of very evident brickwork, which is never fresh or loud in colour, but always burnt out, as it were, always exquisitely mild.

There are certain little mental pictures that rise before the sentimental tourist at the simple mention, written or spoken, of the places he has loved. When I hear, when I see, the magical name I have written above these pages, it is not of the great Square that I think, with its strange basilica and its high arcades, nor of the wide mouth of the Grand Canal, with the stately steps and the well-poised dome of the Salute; it is not of the low lagoon, not the sweet Piazzetta, nor the dark chambers of St Mark's. I simply see a narrow canal in the heart of the city – a patch of green water and a surface of pink wall. The gondola moves slowly; it gives a great, smooth swerve, passes under a bridge, and the gondolier's cry, carried over the quiet water, makes a kind of splash in the stillness. A girl is passing over the little bridge, which has an arch like a camel's back, with an old shawl on her head, which makes her look charming; you see her against the sky as you float beneath. The pink of the old wall seems to fill the whole place; it sinks even into the opaque water. Behind the wall is a garden, out of which the long arm of a white June rose – the roses of Venice are splendid – has flung itself by way of spontaneous ornament. On the other side of this small water-way is a great shabby façade of Gothic windows and balconies – balconies on which dirty clothes are hung and under which a cavernous-looking doorway opens from a low flight of slimy watersteps. It is very hot and still, the canal has a queer smell, and the whole place is enchanting.

HENRY JAMES Portraits of Places, 1883

Santa Maria della Salute

The canal makes a bend, and one sees rising from the water, like some rich marine vegetation, like a splendid and strange piece of whitish coral, Santa Maria della Salute, with its domes, with its accumulation of sculptures, its façade loaded with statues; further off, on another island, San Giorgio Maggiore, all rounded and bristling like a stately shell of mother-of-pearl. One turns one's eyes to the left, and there is St Mark's, the campanile, the square, the Doge's palace. There is probably no jewel its equal in the world.

It cannot be described... There are too many shapes, too vast an accumulation of masterpieces, too great a prodigality of invention... The dominating factor is the wealth and fertility of imagination, the mixture that blends to form a whole, the diversity and contrast which lead to harmony. Imagine eight or ten jewels hanging from a woman's neck, from her arms, and united by their magnificence or by her beauty.

HIPPOLYTE TAINE Voyage en Italie, 1866

Canal Grande

50 Palazzi Salviati,
Barbaro, Dario

Byron in Venice

Some three years ago, or it may be more, I recollect your telling me that you had received a letter from our friend Sam, dated 'On board his gondola'. My gondola is, at this present, waiting for me on the canal; but I prefer writing to you in the house, it being autumn – and rather an English autumn than otherwise. It is my intention to remain at Venice during the winter, probably, as it has always been (next to the East) the greenest island of my imagination. It has not disappointed me; though its evident decay would, perhaps, have that effect upon others. But I have been familiar with ruins too long to dislike desolation. Besides, I have fallen in love, which, next to falling into the canal (which would be of no use, as I can swim) is the best or the worst thing I could do. I have got some extremely good apartments in the house of a 'Merchant of Venice', who is a good deal occupied with business, and has a wife in her twenty-second year.

LORD BYRON to Thomas Moore, 17 November 1816

The Palazzo Mocenigo

I have the Palazzo Mocenigo on the Canal' Grande for three years to come, and a pretty Villa in the Euganean hills for the Summer for nearly the same term.

While I remain in the city itself, I keep my horses on an Island with a good beach, about half a mile from the town, so that I get a gallop of some miles along the shore of the Adriatic daily; the Stables belong to the Fortress, but are let on fair terms.

I was always very partial to Venice, and it has not hitherto disappointed me; but I am not sure that the English in general would like it. I am sure that I should *not*, if *they* did; but, by the benevolence of God, they prefer Florence and Naples, and do not infest us greatly here. In other respects it is very agreeable for Gentlemen of desultory habits – women – wine – and wassail being all extremely fair and reasonable – theatres, etc., good – and Society (after a time) as pleasant as any where else (at least to my mind) if you will live with them in their own way – which is different of course from the Ultramontane in some degree.

The Climate is Italian and that's enough, and the Gondolas, etc., and habits of the place make it like a romance, for it is by no means even now the most regular and correct moral city in the universe. Young and old – pretty and ugly – high and low – are employed in the laudable practice of Lovemaking – and though most Beauty is found amongst the middling and lower classes – this of course only renders their amatory habits more universally diffused.

LORD BYRON to James Wedderburn Webster, 31 May 1818

The Palazzo Rezzonico

I hear from the couple at Venice constantly – from Pen yesterday. They are, within the last few days, lodged in their fine Palazzo: they gave two modest entertainments there by way of house-warming, and were congratulated by everybody on what they had done for Pope Clement XIII – whose apartment they occupy: and it is pleasant to hear how grateful the old Venetian families are at the palace having fallen into such reverent hands – not being destined to vile uses, turned into an hotel, or the like. It is really, on the whole, the best palace in Venice, and has never been modified in the least – except in the trifling business of blocking up windows &c. – all which Pen has carefully restored.

ROBERT BROWNING to George Barrett, 24 February 1889

56 Palazzo Rezzonico

57 Palazzi Mocenigo

58 Palazzo Giustinian, Ca' Foscari

Canal Grande

59
Palazzi Tiepolo,
Pisani-Moretta,
Barbarigo della
Terrazza

60
Palazzi Grimani,
Corner Contarini,
Tron, Volpi

Palaces on the Grand Canal

The City is divided in the middest by a goodly faire channell, which they call Canal il grande. The same is crooked, and made in the form of a Roman S. It is in length a thousand and three hundred paces, and in bredth at the least forty, in some places more. The six parts of the City whereof Venice consisteth, are situate on both sides of this Canal il Grande. The names of them are these, St Marco, Castello, Canareio, that lie on one side of it, and those on the other side are called St Polo, St Croce, Dorso Duro. Also both the sides of this channel are adorned with many sumptuous and magnificent Palaces that stand very neare to the water, and make a very glorious and beautifull shew. For many of them are of a great height three or foure stories high, most being built with bricke, and some few with faire free stone. Besides, they are addorned with a great multitude of stately pillers made partly of white stone, and partly of Istrian marble. Their roofes doe much differ from those of our English buildings. For they are all flat and built in that manner as men may walke upon them, as I have often observed. Which forme of roofing is generally used in all those Italian Cities that I saw, and in some places of France, especially in Lyons, where I could not see as much as one house but had a flat roofe. The like whereof I have read to have beene used in ancient times in Jerusalem, and other Cities of Judæa... Moreover their tiling is done after another manner than ours in England. For they lay it on hollow, but we flat. Many things I observed in these Venetian Palaces, that make them very conspicuous and passing faire; amongst the rest these two things especially. Every Palace of any principall note hath a pretty walke or open gallery betwixt the wall of the house and the brincke of the rivers banke, the edge or extremity whereof is garnished with faire pillars that are finely arched at the top. The walke serveth for men to stand in without their houses, and behold things. Suetonius called these kinde of open galleries Podia. Truly they yeeld no small beauty to their buildings. Againe, I noted another thing in these Venetian Palaces that I have very seldome seen in England, and it is very little used in any other country that I could perceive in my travels, saving only in Venice and other Italian Cities. Somewhat above the middle of the front of the building, or (as I have observed in many of their Palaces) a little beneath the toppe of the front they have right opposite unto their windows, a very pleasant little terrasse, that jutteth or butteth out from the maine building; the edge whereof is decked with many pretty little turned pillers, either of marble or free stone to lean over. These kinde of terrasses or little galleries of pleasure Suetonius calleth Meniana. They give great grace to the whole edifice, and serve only for this purpose, that people may from that place as from a most delectable prospect contemplate and view the parts of the City round about them in the coole evening.

Thomas Coryate Coryat's Crudities, 1611

The bravura style

The Venetians, somewhat behind the rest of Italy in the development of the fine arts, were at the height of prosperity and wealth during the middle period of the Renaissance; and no city is more rich in monuments of the florid style. Something of their own delight in sensuous magnificence they communicated even to the foreigners who dwelt among them. The court of the Ducal Palace, the Scuola di S. Rocco, the Palazzo Corner, and the Palazzo Vendramini-Calergi, illustrate the strong yet fanciful *bravura* style that pleased the aristocracy of Venice. Nowhere else does the architecture of the Middle Ages melt by more imperceptible degrees into that of the Revival, retaining through all changes the impress of a people splendour-loving in the highest sense.

The Library of S. Mark, built by Sansovino in 1536, remains, however, the crowning triumph of Venetian art. It is impossible to contemplate its noble double row of open arches without feeling the eloquence of rhetoric so brilliant, without echoing the judgement of Palladio, that nothing more sumptuous or beautiful had been invented since the age of ancient Rome.

J. A. SYMONDS History of the Renaissance in Italy, 1875–86

The Palazzo Farsetti and Palazzo Loredan

We approach now the Rialto. As soon as we have passed the Casa Grimani, the traveller will recognize, on his right, two rich and extensive masses of building, which form important objects in almost every picturesque view of the noble bridge. Of these, the first, that farthest from the Rialto, retains great part of its ancient materials in a dislocated form. It has been entirely modernized in its upper stories, but the ground floor and the first floor have nearly all their original shafts and capitals…This building is known in Venice as the Casa Farsetti.

The one next to it, though not so conspicuous, and often passed with neglect, will, I believe, be felt at last, by all who examine it carefully, to be the most beautiful palace in the whole extent of the Grand Canal. It has been restored often, once in the Gothic, once in the Renaissance times… The Gothic additions harmonize exquisitely with its Byzantine work, and it is easy, as we examine its lovely central arcade, to forget the Renaissance additions which encumber it above. It is known as the Casa Loredan.

JOHN RUSKIN The Stones of Venice, 1851–53

The Rialto Bridge

The best building raised in the time of the Grotesque Renaissance; very noble in its simplicity, in its proportions, and in its masonry. Note especially the grand way in which the oblique archstones rest on the butments of the bridge, safe, palpably both to the sense and eye: note also the sculpture of the Annunciation on the southern side of it: how beautifully arranged, so as to give more lightness and grace to the arch...

The bridge was built by Antonio da Ponte, in 1588. It was anciently of wood, with drawbridges in the centre, a representation of which may be seen in one of Carpaccio's pictures at the Accademia delle Belle Arti: and the traveller should observe that the interesting effect, both of this and the Bridge of Sighs, depends in great part on their both being *more* than bridges; the one a covered passage, the other a row of shops, sustained on an arch.

JOHN RUSKIN The Stones of Venice, 1851–53

61 Canal Grande, Vista dal Ponte di Rialto

65 Ponte
di Rialto

Canal Grande

66 Palazzo dei Camerlenghi

67 Fondaco dei Tedeschi

68 Fondaco dei Turchi

Once proud Venice

How strange, yet how beautiful was the first view of Venice! It seemed in the distance like a floating city, its domes, spires, cupolas, and towers, glittering in the sunbeams, and looked so glorious, that I could have fancied it one of those optical illusions presented by a mirage. As we entered the grand canal, the reality of the scene became impressed on my mind, and the grandeur of the houses, with the rich and solid architectural decorations lavished on them, formed so striking and melancholy a contrast to the ruin into which they are fast falling, that the scene was awakened feelings of deep sadness in my breast. The palaces looked as if the touch of some envious wizard had caused them to decay, long ere Time the destroyer would have scathed them; and this premature ruin has in it something much more mournful than that gradually effected by the lapse of years. Windows whose architraves are supported by caryatides of exquisite sculpture, are blocked up in the rudest manner; and out of them protrude the iron pipes of German stoves, sending forth their murky vapours to the blue and cloudless sky whose purity they profane. Over balustrades of marble, where once beauty loved to lean, float the unseemly nether garments suspended to be dried, of the Teutonic inhabitants who now fill those sculptured dwellings with the mingled odours of cigars and garlick; and mutter the guttural sounds of their language, where once the dulcet tones of the softest of all the Italian dialects, were wont to be heard.

The canal, too, over which our boat glided, bore evidence of the fallen state of the once proud Venice, for a green opaque slimy substance half-choked its water, sending out a most unsavory smell, as the oars disturbed its unhealthy deposits. Alas! like anticipated happiness which looks so bright at a distance and loses its charms when approached, Venice, when entered disappoints, and inspires only gloomy reflections; its very beauty rendering its decay more painful to be witnessed.

The gondolas with their funereal trappings, dashing by us, over the opaque water, looked as if freighted with the dead owners of the half-dismantled palaces we passed, so lugubrious are their appearance: but this very sombreness is in harmony with all around, for aught of gay, or brilliant, would offer too violent a contrast to the scene. The very brightness of the azure sky above this fast decaying, yet still magnificent city, renders its aspect more touching; and one feels disposed to turn from it with much of the same emotion with which we would shut out the garish sun, when its beams fall on the coffin of one beloved, while it is journeying to the grave.

Venice more than realizes my expectations, though they were highly excited by all that I had read, and by the pictures of Canaletti. But even these last, though accurate representations of the spots portrayed, fall short in conveying a just notion of their beauty; so much does the reality gain by the clearness of the atmosphere, and by the strong and beautiful contrasts of the surrounding light and shade.

LADY BLESSINGTON The Idler in Italy, 1839–40

The market

Amongst many other things that moved great admiration in me in Venice, this was not the least, to consider the marveilous affluence and exuberancy of all things tending to the sustentation of mans life. For albeit they have neyther meadows, nor pastures, nor arable grounds neare their city (which is matter impossible, because it is seated in the sea, and distinguished with such a multitude of channels) to yeeld them corne and victuals: yet they have as great abundance (a thing very strang to be considered) of victuals, corne and fruites of all sorts whatsoever, as any city (I thinke) of all Italy. Their victuals and all other provision being very plenteously ministred unto them from Padua, Vicenza, and other bordering townes and places of Lombardy, which are in their owne dominion. For I have seene their shambles and market places (whereof they have a great multitude) exceedingly well furnished with all manner of necessaries. As for their fruits I have observed wonderful plenty amongst them, as Grapes, Peares, Apples, Plummes, Apricockes: all which are sold by weight, and not by tale: Figges most excellent of three or foure sorts, as blacke, which are the daintiest, greene, and yellow. Likewise they had another special commodity when I was there, which is one of the most delectable dishes for a Sommer fruite of all Christendome, namely muske Melons. I wondered at the plenty of them; for there was such store brought into the citie every morning and evening for the space of a moneth together, that not onely St Markes place, but also all the market places of the citie were super-abundantly furnished with them; insomuch that I thinke there were sold so many of them every day for that space, as yeelded five hundred pound sterling. They are of three sorts, yellow, greene, and redde, but the red is most toothsome of all. The great long banke whereof I have before spoken, which is interjected as a strong Rampier betweixt the Adriatique sea and the citie, even the Litto maggior, doth yeeld the greatest store of these Melons that are brought to Venice. But I advise thee (gentle Reader) if thou meanest to see Venice, and shall happen to be there in the sommer time when they are ripe, to abstaine from the immoderate eating of them. For the sweetnesse of them is such as hath allured many men to eate so immoderately of them, that they have therewith hastened their untimely death: the fruite being sweete-sowre. Sweete in the palate, but sowre in the stomacke, if it be not soberly eaten. For it doth often breede the Dysenteria, that is, the bloudy fluxe: of which disease the Emperour Fredericke the third died by the intemperate eating of them, as I will hereafter declare in my observations of Germany. Also they have another excellent fruite called Anguria, the coldest fruit in taste that ever I did eate: the pith of it, which is in the middle, is as redde as blood, and full of blacke kernels. They finde a notable commodity of it in sommer, for the cooling of themselves in time of heate. For it hath the most refrigerating vertue of all the fruites in Italy. Moreover the abundance of fish, which is twise a day brought into the citie, is so great, that they have not onely exceeding plenty for themselves, but also doe communicate that commodity to their neighbour townes. Amongst many other strang fishes that I have observed in their market places, I have seene many Torteises, whereof I never saw but one in all England. Besides they have great plenty of fowle, and such admirable variety thereof, that I have heard in the citie they are furnished with no lesse then two hundred severall sortes of them. I have observed a thing amongst the Venetians, that I have not a little wondred at, that their Gentlemen and greatest Senators, a man worth perhaps two millions of duckats, will come into the market, and buy their flesh, fish, fruites, and such other things as are necessary for the maintenance of their family; a token indeed of frugality, which is commendable in all men; but me thinkes it is not an argument of true generosity, that a noble spirit should deject it selfe to these petty and base matters, that are fitter to be done by servants than men of a generose parentage. Therefore I commend mine owne country-men, the English Gentleman, that scorneth to goe into the market to buy his victuals and other necessaries for house-keeping, but employeth his Cooke or Cator about those inferior and sordid affaires.

THOMAS CORYATE Coryat's Crudities, 1611

73, 75 Gondolieri

74 Traghetto di S. Sofia

The thirteen ferries

There are in Venice thirteen ferries or passages, which they commonly call Traghetti, where passengers may be transported in a Gondola to what place of the City they will. Of which thirteene, one is under this Rialto bridge. But the boatmen that attend at this ferry are the most vicious and licentious varlets about all the City. For if a stranger entereth into one of their Gondolas, and doth not presently tell them whither he will goe, they will incontinently carry him of their owne accord to a religious house forsooth, where his plumes shall be well pulled before he commeth forth againe. Then he may afterward with Demosthenes buy too dear repentance for seeing Lais, except he doth for that time either with Ulysses stop his eares, or with Democritus pull out his eyes. Therefore I counsaile all my countrimen whatsoever, Gentlemen or others that determine hereafter to see Venice, to beware of the Circæan cups, and the Syrens melody, I meane these seducing and tempting Gondoleers of the Rialto bridge, least they afterward cry Peccavi when it is to late. For

> facilis descensus Averni,
> Noctes atque dies patet atri janua Ditis.

Besides they shall finde the iniquity of them to be such, that if the passenger commandeth them to carry him to any place where his serious and urgent businesse lies, which he cannot but follow without some prejudice unto him, these impious miscreants will either strive to carry him away, maugre his hart, to some irreligious place whether he would not goe, or at the least tempt him with their diabolicall perswasions.

THOMAS CORYATE Coryat's Crudities, 1611

109

The mysterious impersonality of the gondola

There is something strange and fascinating in this mysterious impersonality of the gondola. It has an identity when you are in it, but, thanks to their all being of the same size, shape, and colour, and of the same deportment and gait, it has none, or as little as possible, as you see it pass before you. From my windows on the Riva there was always the same silhouette – the long, black, slender skiff, lifting its head and throwing it back a little, moving yet seeming not to move, with the grotesquely-graceful figure on the poop. This figure inclines, as may be, more to the graceful or to the grotesque – standing in the 'second position' of the dancing-master, but indulging, from the waist upward, in a freedom of movement which that functionary would deprecate. One may say, as a general thing, that there is something rather awkward in the movement of even the most graceful gondolier, and something graceful in the movement of the most awkward. In the graceful men of course the grace predominates, and nothing can be finer than the large firm way in which, from their point of vantage, they throw themselves over their tremendous oar. It has the boldness of a plunging bird, and the regularity of a pendulum. Sometimes, as you see this movement in profile, in a gondola that passes you – as you recline on your own low cushions, the arching body of the gondolier lifted up against the sky – it has a kind of nobleness which suggest an image on a Greek frieze. The gondolier at Venice is your very good friend – if you choose him happily – and on the quality of the personage depends a good deal of your impressions. He is a part of your daily life, your double, your shadow, your complement. Most people, I think, either like their gondolier or hate him; and if they like him, like him very much.

HENRY JAMES Portraits of Places, 1883

The singing gondolier

We reached Venice at eight in the evening, and entered a hearse belonging to the Grand Hotel d'Europe. At any rate, it was more like a hearse than anything else, though to speak by the card, it was a gondola. And this was the storied gondola of Venice! – the fairy boat in which the princely cavaliers of the olden time were wont to cleave the waters of the moonlit canals and look the eloquence of love into the soft eyes of patrician beauties, while the gay gondolier in silken doublet touched his guitar and sang as only gondoliers can sing! This the famed gondola and this the gorgeous gondolier! – the one an inky, rusty old canoe with a sable hearse-body clapped on to the middle of it, and the other a mangy, barefooted gutter-snipe with a portion of his raiment on exhibition which should have been sacred from public scrutiny. Presently, as he turned a corner and shot his hearse into a dismal ditch between two long rows of towering, untenanted buildings, the gay gondolier began to sing, true to the traditions of his race. I stood it a little while. Then I said:

'Now, here, Roderigo Gonzales Michael Angelo, I'm a pilgrim, and I'm a stranger, but I am not going to have my feelings lacerated by any such caterwauling as that. If that goes on, one of us has got to take water. It is enough that my cherished dreams of Venice have been blighted forever as to the romantic gondola and the gorgeous gondolier; this system of destruction shall go no farther; I will accept the hearse, under protest, and you may fly your flag of truce in peace, but here I register a dark and bloody oath that you shan't sing. Another yelp, and overboard you go.'

I began to feel that the old Venice of song and story had departed forever. But I was too hasty. In a few minutes we swept gracefully out into the Grand Canal, and under the mellow moonlight the Venice of poetry and romance stood revealed. Right from the water's edge rose long lines of stately palaces of marble; gondolas were gliding swiftly hither and thither and disappearing suddenly through unsuspected gates and alleys; ponderous stone bridges threw their shadows athwart the glittering waves. There was life and motion everywhere, and yet everywhere there was a hush, a stealthy sort of stillness, that was suggestive of secret enterprises of bravoes and of lovers; and, clad half in moonbeams and half in mysterious shadows, the grim old mansions of the republic seemed to have an expression about them of having an eye out for just such enterprises as these at that same moment. Music came floating over the waters –Venice was complete.

MARK TWAIN The Innocents Abroad, 1869

The charms of evening

Of all dreamy delights, that of floating in a gondola along the canals and out on the Lagoon is surely the greatest. We were out one night on the Lagoon when the sun was setting, and the wide waters were flushed with the reddened light. I should have liked it to last for hours: it is the sort of scene in which I could most readily forget my own existence, and feel melted into the general life.

Another charm of evening time was to walk up and down the Piazza of San Marco as the stars were brightening and look at the grand dim buildings, and the flocks of pigeons flitting about them; or to walk on to the Bridge of La Paglia and look along the dark canal that runs under the Bridge of Sighs –its blackness lit up by a gaslight here and there, and the plash of the oar of blackest gondola slowly advancing.

GEORGE ELIOT's Life, 1885

112

77 Palazzo Pesar

80

81 Canal Grande, S. Geremia, Palazzo Labia

84 Scuola Grande di S. Rocco

85 S. Rocco

6 S. Maria Gloriosa
dei Frari

Andrea Verrocchio

The name of Verrocchio is best known to the world through the equestrian statue of Bartolomeo Colleoni. When this great Condottiere, the last surviving general trained by Braccio da Montone, died in 1475, he bequeathed a large portion of his wealth to Venice, on condition that his statue on horseback should be erected in the Piazza di S. Marco. Colleoni, having long held the bâton of the Republic, desired that after death his portrait, in his habit as he lived, should continue to look down on the scene of his old splendour. By an ingenious quibble the Senators adhered to the letter of his will without infringing a law that forbade them to charge the square of S. Mark with monuments. They ruled that the piazza in front of the Scuola di S. Marco, better known as the Campo di S. Zanipolo, might be chosen as the site of Colleoni's statue, and to Andrea Verrocchio was given the commission for its erection.

Andrea died in 1488 before the model for the horse was finished. The work was completed and the pedestal was supplied by Alessandro Leopardi. To Verrocchio, profiting by the example of Donatello's 'Gattamelata', must be assigned the general conception of this statue; but the breath of life that animates both horse and rider, the richness of detail that enhances the massive grandeur of the group, and the fiery spirit of its style of execution were due to the Venetian genius of Leopardi. Verrocchio alone produced nothing so truly magnificent. This joint creation of Florentine science and Venetian fervour is one of the most precious monuments of the Renaissance. From it we learn what the men who fought the bloodless battles of the commonwealths, and who aspired to principality, were like. 'He was tall,' writes a biographer of Colleoni, 'of erect and well-knit figure, and of well-proportioned limbs. His complexion tended rather to brown, marked withal by bright and sanguine flesh-tints. He had black eyes; their brilliancy was vivid, their gaze terrible and penetrating.

In the outline of his nose and in all his features he displayed a manly nobleness com-
bined with goodness and prudence.' Better phrases cannot be chosen to describe his
statue.

J. A. SYMONDS History of the Renaissance in Italy, 1875–86

The Colleoni Statue

To make the statue Verrocchio came to Venice, and had just modelled the horse,
when a report reached him that the Signory intended to have the rider executed by
Donatello's scholar, Vellano of Padua. Indignant at this intended insult, he instantly
broke the head and legs of the horse in pieces, and returned to Florence, whither he
was followed by a decree forbidding him under pain of death again to set foot upon
Venetian territory; to which he replied, that he never would incur that risk, as he
was aware that if his head were once cut off, the Signory could neither put it on
again nor supply its place, while he could at any time replace the head of his horse
by a better one. Feeling the truth of this answer, the Venetians rescinded their unjust
edict, and not only invited Verrocchio to resume his work, but doubled his pay,
and pledged themselves not to allow him to be in any way interfered with. Pacified
by this *amende honorable,* he returned to Venice, and had begun to restore his broken
model, when he was attacked by a violent illness which speedily carried him to his
grave. How much, or rather how little, of his task was then completed, is clearly shown
by the passage of his will in which he supplicates the Signory to allow his scholar
Lorenzo di Credi, to finish the horse which he had commenced. His request was not
complied with, and Alessandro Leopardi, a Venetian sculptor, was employed to complete the group, but, as he doubtless used Verrocchio's sketches, the general conception must be ascribed to the latter; though as we look upon this rich and picturesque
group, whose ample forms are so opposed to the meagreness of the Tuscan sculptor's
manner, we are led to conclude that Leopardi worked out Verrocchio's idea accord-

ing to his own taste, and honour him as the chief author of this, the finest modern equestrian statue, as did the Venetians, by giving him the surname 'del Cavallo'.

The stalwart figure of Colleoni, clad in armour with a helmet upon his head, is the most perfect embodiment of the idea which history gives us of an Italian Condottiere. As his horse, with arched neck and slightly bent head, paces slowly forward, he, sitting straight in his saddle, turns to look over his left shoulder, showing us a sternly marked countenance, with deep-set eyes, whose intensity of expression reveals a character of iron which never recoiled before any obstacle... The stern simplicity of the rider is happily set off by the richness of detail lavished upon the saddle, the breast-plate, the crupper, and the knotted mane of his steed; and the effect of the whole group is heightened by the very elegant pedestal upon which Leopardi has placed it.

CHARLES CALLAHAN PERKINS Tuscan Sculptors, 1864

The splendour of light and colour

Nowhere (not even in Holland, where the correspondence between the real aspects and the little polished canvases is so constant and so exquisite) do art and life seem so interfused and, as it were, so consanguineous. All the splendour of light and colour, all the Venetian air and the Venetian history, are on the walls and ceilings of the palaces; and all the genius of the masters, all the images and vision they have left upon canvas, seem to tremble in the sunbeams and dance upon the waves. That is the perpetual interest of the place – that you live in a certain sort of knowledge as in a rosy cloud. You don't go into the churches and galleries by way of a change from the streets; you go into them because they offer you an exquisite reproduction of the things that surround you. All Venice was both model and painter, and life was so pictorial that art could not help becoming so.

HENRY JAMES Portraits of Places, 1883

The Byzantine influence

So soon as the classical enthusiasm required the banishment of the Gothic forms, it was natural that the Venetian mind should turn back with affection to the Byzantine models in which the round arches and simple shafts, necessitated by recent law, were presented under a form consecrated by the usage of their ancestors. And, accordingly, the first distinct school of architecture which arose under the new dynasty, was one in which the method of inlaying marble, and the general forms of shaft and arch, were adopted from the buildings of the twelfth century, and applied with the utmost possible refinements of modern skill...

The two most refined buildings in this style in Venice are the small Church of the Miracoli, and the Scuola di San Marco beside the church of St John and St Paul. The noblest is the Rio Façade of the Ducal Palace. The Casa Dario, and the Casa Manzoni, on the Grand Canal, are exquisite examples of the school, as applied to domestic architecture; and, in the reach of the canal between the Casa Foscari and the Rialto, there are several palaces, of which the Casa Contarini (called 'delle Figure') is the principal, belonging to the same group, though somewhat later, and as remarkable for the association of the Byzantine principles of colour with the severest lines of the Roman pediment, gradually superseding the round arch. The precision of chiselling and delicacy of proportion in the ornament and general lines of these palaces cannot be too highly praised; and I believe that the traveller in Venice, in general, gives them rather too little attention than too much.

JOHN RUSKIN The Stones of Venice, 1851–53

89

91

90

92

95 Teatro La Fenice

Gondolas, pigeons and the plague

Anyone... who has become enamoured of the lagoons and lagoon life will find himself obliged to make friends with the gondola. That is no difficult task, for it is an historical vessel, unique in itself, and a constant source of admiration and surprise, as one sees its great length obeying the impulse of its single rower, who guides it with a skill that takes rank as a fine art. It is the most charming carriage in the world, and so thoroughly Venetian that Venice would hardly be Venice without it... Through centuries of experience the boat has been fashioned and modified, until at length, it has achieved the union of beauty, ease and usefulness. The long, black skiff, with its graceful lines, its swanlike prow sweeping up from the water, and its gliding movement, is a dear and lovely feature, the most familiar in the city of the sea.

In Venice the pigeons do not allow you to forget them, even if one desired to forget a bird that is so intimately connected with the city and with a great ceremony of that ancient Republic which has passed away. They belong so entirely to the place, and especially to the great square; they have made their home for so many generations among the carvings of the Basilica, at the feet of the bronze horses, and under the massive cornices of the New Procuratie, that the great campanile itself is hardly more essential to the character of the Piazza than are these delicate denizens of Saint Mark's. In the structure of the ducal palace the wants of the pigeons have been taken into account, and near the two great wells which stand in the inner courtyard little cups of Istrian stone have been let into the pavement for the pigeons to drink from. On cold, frosty mornings you may see them tapping disconsolately at the ice which covers their drinking troughs, and may win their thanks by breaking it for them. Or if the *borin* blows from the east, the pigeons sit in long rows under the eaves of the Procuratie; their necks drawn into the shoulders, and the neck feathers ruffled round their heads, till they have lost all shape, and look like a row of slate-coloured cannon-balls.

Venice has never forgotten to be grateful to 'Mary the Mother of Health' who freed her from her last great plague. Every year, on the 21st of November, thanksgiving services are held in the Church of the Salute, whose group of cupolas and fanciful buttresses and statues form such a wilful and picturesque object, standing, as they do, on the point of the Dogana, and opposite the graver façade of Palladio's San Giorgio. The church was built in quittance of a vow made to the Virgin if she would save the city from the plague. The pestilence had raged for sixteen months, destroying eighty-two thousand people in Venice and the neighbouring islands. It stopped suddenly in November of the year 1631, as the winter drew on. The public prayers had apparently been answered, and the vow of the Senate accepted. The joy was boundless, for this plague had been the most terrible of all the seventy which, up to that date, had desolated Venice.

HORATIO F. BROWN Life on the Lagoons, 1884

A city for beavers

I am speedily satisfied with Venice. It is a great oddity, a city for beavers, but, to my thought, a most disagreeable residence. You feel always in prison, and solitary.

RALPH WALDO EMERSON Journal, June, 1883

The sentimental tourist

It is possible to dislike Venice, and to entertain the sentiment in a responsible and intelligent manner. There are travellers who think the place odious, and those who are not of this opinion often find themselves wishing that the others were only more numerous. The sentimental tourist's only quarrel with his Venice is that he has too many competitors there. He likes to be alone; to be original; to have (to himself, at least) the air of making discoveries. The Venice of to-day is a vast museum where the little wicket that admits you is perpetually turning and creaking, and you march through the institution with a herd of fellow-gazers. There is nothing left to discover or describe, and originality of attitude is completely impossible. This is often very annoying; you can only turn your back on your impertinent play-fellow and curse his want of delicacy. But this is not the fault of Venice; it is the fault of the rest of the world. The fault of Venice is that, though it is easy to admire it, is not so easy to live in it. After you have been there a week, and the bloom of novelty has rubbed off, you wonder whether you can accommodate yourself to the peculiar conditions ...

You have begun to have a shipboard-feeling — to regard the Piazza as an enormous saloon and the Riva degli Schiavoni as a promenade-deck. You are obstructed and encaged; your desire for space is unsatisfied; you miss your usual exercise. You try to take a walk, and you fail, and meantime, as I say, you have come to regard your gondola as a sort of magnified baby's cradle.

The canals have a horrible smell, and the everlasting Piazza, where you have looked repeatedly at every article in every shop-window and found them all rubbish, where the young Venetians who sell bead-bracelets and 'panoramas' are perpetually thrusting their wares at you, where the same tightly-buttoned officers are for ever sucking the same black weeds, at the same empty tables, in front of the same caffès – the Piazza, as I say, has resolved itself into a sort of magnificent tread-mill. This is the state of mind of those shallow inquirers who find Venice all very well for a week; and if in such a state of mind you take your departure, you act with fatal rashness. The loss is your own, moreover; it is not – with all deference to your personal attractions – that of your companions who remain behind; for though there are some disagreeable things in Venice, there is nothing so disagreeable as the visitors.

The place is as changeable as a nervous woman, and you know it only when you know all the aspects of its beauty. It has high spirits or low, it is pale or red, gray or pink, cold or warm, fresh or wan, according to the weather or the hour. It is always interesting and almost always sad; but it has a thousand occasional graces and is always liable to happy accidents.

Fortunately for the present proser, the weather was not always fine; the first month was wet and windy, and it was better to look at the lagoon from an open casement than to respond to the advances of persuasive gondoliers. Even then, however, there was a constant entertainment in the view. It was all cold colour, and the steel-gray floor of the lagoon was stroked the wrong way by the wind. Then there were charming cool intervals, when the churches, the houses, the anchored fishing-boats, the whole gently-curving line of the Riva, seemed to be washed with a pearly white. Later it all turned warm – warm to the eye as well as to other senses. After the middle of May the whole place was in a glow. The sea took on a thousand shades, but they were only infinite variations of blue, and those rosy walls I just spoke of began to flush in the thick sunshine. Every patch of colour, every yard of weather-stained stucco, every glimpse of nestling garden or daub of sky above a *calle*, began to shine and sparkle – began, as the painters say, to 'compose'. The lagoon was streaked with odd currents, which played across it like huge, smooth finger-marks. The gondolas multiplied and spotted it all over; every gondola and every gondolier looking, at a distance, precisely like every other.

HENRY JAMES Portraits of Places, 1883

101 Fondamenta
dell'Osmarin

102
Campo S. Provolo

103 Palazzo
Contarini
del Bovolo

An Italian dream

I was awakened after some time (as I thought) by the stopping of the coach. It was now quite night, and we were at the waterside. There lay here a black boat, with a little house or cabin in it of the same mournful colour. When I had taken my seat in this, the boat was paddled, by two men, towards a great light lying in the distance on the sea.

Ever and again there was a dismal sigh of wind. It ruffled the water, and rocked the boat, and sent the dark clouds flying before the stars. I could not but think how strange it was to be floating away at that hour: leaving the land behind, and going on towards this light upon the sea. It soon began to burn brighter; and, from being one light, became a cluster of tapers, twinkling and shining out of the water, as the boat approached towards them by a dreamy kind of track, marked out upon the sea by posts and piles.

We had floated on, five miles or so, over the dark water, when I heard it rippling, in my dream, against some obstruction near at hand. Looking out attentively, I saw, through the gloom, a something black and massive – like a shore, but lying close and flat upon the water, like a raft – which we were gliding past. The chief of the two rowers said it was a burial-place.

Full of the interest and wonder which a cemetery lying out there, in the lonely sea, inspired, I turned to gaze upon it as it should recede in our path, when it was quickly shut out from my view. Before I knew by what, or how, I found that we were gliding up a street – a phantom street; the houses rising on both sides from the water, and the black boat gliding on beneath their windows. Lights were shining from some of these casements, plumbing the depth of the black stream with their reflected rays; but all was profoundly silent.

So we advanced into this ghostly city, continuing to hold our course through narrow streets and lanes, all filled and flowing with water. Some of the corners where our way branched off were so acute and narrow, that it seemed impossible for the long slender boat to turn them; but the rowers, with a low, melodious cry of warning, sent it skimming on without a pause. Sometimes the rowers of another black boat like our own echoed the cry, and, slackening their speed (as I thought we did ours), would come flitting past us, like a dark shadow. Other boats of the same sombre hue, were lying moored, I thought, to painted pillars, near to dark, mysterious doors that opened straight upon the water. Some of these were empty; in some the rowers lay asleep; towards one I saw some figures coming down a gloomy archway from the interior of a palace: gaily dressed, and attended by torch-bearers. It was but a glimpse I had of them; for a bridge so low and close upon the boat that it seemed ready to fall down and crush us: one of the many bridges that perplexed the Dream: blotted them out instantly. On we went, floating towards the heart of this strange place—with water all about us where never water was elsewhere—clusters of houses, churches, heaps of stately buildings growing out of it—and everywhere, the same extraordinary silence. Presently, we shot across a broad and open stream; and passing, as I thought, before a spacious paved quay, where the bright lamps with which it was illuminated showed long rows of arches and pillars, of ponderous construction and great strength, but as light to the eye as garlands of hoar frost or gossamer—and where, for the first time, I saw people walking—arrived at a flight of steps leading from the water to a large mansion, where, having passed through corridors and galleries innumerable, I lay down to rest; listening to the black boats stealing up and down below the window on the rippling water till I fell asleep.

The glory of the day that broke upon me in this Dream; its freshness, motion, buoyancy; its sparkles of the sun in water; its clear blue sky and rustling air; no waking words can tell. But, from my window, I looked down on boats and barks; on masts, sails, cordage, flags; on groups of busy sailors working at the cargoes of these vessels; on wide quays strewn with bales, casks, merchandise of many kinds; on great ships lying near at hand in stately indolence; on islands crowned with gorgeous domes and turrets; and where golden crosses glittered in the light, atop of wondrous churches springing from the sea! Going down upon the margin of the green sea, rolling on before the door, and filling all the streets, I came upon a place of such surpassing beauty, and such grandeur, that all the rest was poor and faded, in comparison with its absorbing loveliness.

It was a great Piazza, as I thought; anchored, like all the rest, in the deep ocean. On its broad bosom was a Palace, more majestic and magnificent in its old age than all the buildings of the earth, in the high prime and fulness of their youth. Cloisters and galleries: so light, they might have been the work of fairy hands: so strong, that centuries had battered them in vain: wound round and round this palace, and enfolded it with a Cathedral, gorgeous in the wild luxuriant fancies of the East. At no great distance from its porch, a lofty tower standing by itself, and rearing its proud head, alone, into the sky, looked out upon the Adriatic Sea. Near to the margin of the stream were two ill-omened pillars of red granite; one having on its top a figure with a sword and shield; the other, a winged lion. Not far from these, again, a second tower: richest of the rich in all its decorations: even here, where all was rich: sustained aloft a great orb, gleaming with gold and deepest blue: the Twelve Signs painted on it, and a mimic sun revolving in its course around them: while above, two bronze giants hammered out the hours upon a sounding bell. An oblong square of lofty houses of the whitest stone, surrounded by a light and beautiful arcade, formed part of this enchanted scene; and, here and there, gay masts for flags rose, tapering from the pavement of the unsubstantial ground.

I thought I entered the Cathedral, and went in and out among its many arches: traversing its whole extent. A grand and dreamy structure of immense proportions; golden with old mosaics; redolent of perfumes; dim with the smoke of incense; costly in treasure of precious stones and metals, glittering through iron bars; holy with the bodies of deceased saints; rainbow-hued with windows of stained glass; dark with carved woods and coloured marbles; obscure in its vast heights and lengthened distances; shining with silver lamps and winking lights; unreal, fantastic, solemn, inconceivable throughout. I thought I entered the old palace; pacing silent galleries and council-chambers, where the old rulers of this mistress of the waters looked sternly out, in pictures, from the walls, and where her high-prowed galleys, still victorious on canvas, fought and conquered as of old. I thought I wandered through its halls of state and triumph – bare and empty now! – and musing on its pride and might, extinct: for that was past; all past: heard a voice say, 'Some tokens of its ancient rule, and some consoling reason for its downfall, may be traced here yet!'

I dreamed that I was led on, then into some jealous rooms, communicating with a prison near the palace; separated from it by a lofty bridge crossing a narrow street; and called, I dreamed, The Bridge of Sighs.

But first I passed two jagged slits in a stone wall; the lions' mouths – now toothless – where, in the distempered horror of my sleep, I thought denunciations of innocent men to the old wicked Council had been dropped through, many a time, when the night was dark. So, when I saw the council-room to which such prisoners were taken for examination, and the door by which they passed out when they were condemned – a door that never closed upon a man with life and hope before him – my heart appeared to die within me.

It was smitten harder though, when, torch in hand, I descended from the cheerful day into two ranges, one below another, of dismal, awful, horrible stone cells. They were quite dark. Each had a loophole in its massive wall, where, in the old time, every day, a torch was placed – I dreamed – to light the prisoner within for half an hour. The captives, by the glimmering of these brief rays, had scratched and cut inscriptions in the blackened vaults. I saw them. For their labour with a rusty nail's point had outlived their agony and them, through many generations.

One cell I saw, in which no man remained for more than four-and-twenty hours; being marked for dead before he entered it. Hard by, another, and a dismal one, whereto, at midnight, the confessor came – a monk brown-robed, and hooded – ghastly in the day, and free bright air, but in the midnight of that murky prison, Hope's extinguisher, and Murder's herald. I had my foot upon the spot where, at the same dread hour, the shriven prisoner was strangled; and struck my hand upon the guilty door – low-browed and stealthy – through which the lumpish sack was carried out into a boat, and rowed away, and drowned where it was death to cast a net.

Around this dungeon stronghold, and above some part of it: licking the rough walls without, and smearing them with damp and slime within: stuffing dank weeds and refuse into chinks and crevices, as if the very stones and bars had mouths to stop: furnishing a smooth road for the removal of the bodies of the secret victims of the state – a road so ready that it went along with them, and ran before them, like a cruel officer – flowed the same water that filled this Dream of mine, and made it seem one, even at the time.

Descending from the palace by a staircase, called, I thought, the Giant's – I had some imaginary recollection of an old man abdicating, coming, more slowly and more feebly, down it, when he heard the bell proclaiming his successor – I glided off, in one of the dark boats, until we came to an old arsenal guarded by four marble lions. To make my Dream more monstrous and unlikely, one of these had words and sentences upon its body, inscribed there at an unknown time, and in an unknown language; so that their purport was a mystery to all men...

Sometimes, alighting at the doors of churches and vast palaces, I wandered on, from room to room, from aisle to aisle, through labyrinths of rich altars, ancient monuments; decayed apartments where the furniture, half awful, half grotesque, was mouldering away. Pictures were there, replete with such enduring beauty and expression: with such passion, truth, and power: that they seemed so many young and fresh realities among a host of spectres. I thought these often intermingled with the old days of the city: with its beauties, tyrants, captains, patriots, merchants, courtiers, priests: nay, with its very stones, and bricks, and public places; all of which lived again, about me, on the walls. Then coming down some marble staircase where the water lapped and oozed against the lower steps, I passed into my boat again, and went on in my dream.

Floating down narrow lanes, where carpenters, at work with plane and chisel in their shops, tossed the light shaving straight upon the water, where it lay like weed, or ebbed away before me in a tangled heap. Past open doors, decayed and rotten from long steeping in the wet, through which some scanty patch of vine shone green and bright, making unusual shadows on the pavement with its trembling leaves. Past quays and terraces, where women, gracefully veiled, were passing and repassing, and where idlers were reclining in the sunshine, on flagstones and on flights of steps. Past bridges, where there were idlers too: loitering and looking over. Below stone balconies, erected at a giddy height before the loftiest windows of the loftiest houses. Past plots of garden theatres, shrines, prodigious piles of architecture – Gothic – Saracenic – fanciful with all the fancies of all times and countries. Past buildings that were high and low, and black, and white, and straight, and crooked; mean and grand, crazy and strong. Twinging among a tangled lot of boats and barges, and shooting out at last into a Grand Canal! There, in the errant fancy of my dream, I saw old Shylock passing to and fro upon a bridge, all built upon with shops and humming with the tongues of men; a form I seemed to know for Desdemona's, leaned down through a latticed blind to pluck a flower. And, in the dream, I thought that Shakespeare's spirit was abroad upon the water somewhere: stealing through the city.

At night, when two votive lamps burnt before an image of the Virgin, in a gallery outside the great cathedral, near the roof, I fancied that the great piazza of the Winged Lion was a blaze of cheerful light, and that its whole arcade was thronged with people; while crowds were diverting themselves in splendid coffee-houses opening from it – which were never shut, I thought, but open all night long. When the bronze giants struck the hour of midnight on the bell, I thought the life and animation of the city were all centred here; and as I rowed away, abreast the silent quays, I only saw them dotted, here and there, with sleeping boatmen wrapped up in their cloaks, and lying at full length upon the stones.

But, close about the quays and churches, palaces and prisons: sucking at their walls, and welling up into the secret places of the town: crept the water always. Noiseless and watchful: coiled round and round it, in its many folds, like an old serpent: waiting for the time, I thought, when people should look down into its depths for any stone of the old city that had claimed to be its mistress.

Thus it floated me away, until I awoke in the old Marketplace at Verona. I have, many and many a time, thought since of this strange Dream upon the water: half wondering if it lie there yet, and if its name be Venice.

CHARLES DICKENS Pictures from Italy, 1846

107

108

False, lying, thieving rascals

I wish you were here in Venice, there are so many pleasant people amongst the Italians that it would melt a man's heart. Scholars, good lute-players, pipers, men with an understanding of painting and many of noble spirit, right virtuous persons and they show me much honour and friendship. On the other hand there are also the most false, lying, thieving rascals that may be found, I think, anywhere in the world. And if a man did not know this, he would think them the most pleasant people on earth. I am fain to laugh when they converse with me. They know well that their wickedness is known, but they do not care. I have many good friends among the Italians who warn me that I should not eat or drink with their painters. I also have many enemies who talk scornfully of my work in the church and wherever they come across it. Afterwards they run it down, and say that it is not in the style of the ancients and therefore is not good. But Giovanni Bellini has praised me highly in front of many noblemen.

I shall have finished here in ten days' time. Then I wish to ride to Bologna, for art's sake, where a man is to teach me the secrets of perspective. I shall stay there about eight or ten days before I ride back to Venice. From there I shall take the next courier. Oh, how I shall long for the sun! – here I am a gentleman, at home a parasite.

ALBRECHT DÜRER to Willibald Pirckheimer, 1506

The merchants

Item, may you and yours enjoy many prosperous, happy years. Your devoted servant, dear Herr Pirckheimer. As to my health, I pray God to grant you much better. Item, inasmuch as you noted down certain pearls and precious stones that I should purchase, you shall learn that I can obtain none that are good or worth the price, all is snapped up by the Germans. Those that trade along the *Riva* look always to gain fourfold; they are the falsest people who dwell there. No man may look to any one of them for any true service. Therefore, certain other worthy fellows warned me to beware of them, they respect neither God nor man, one can buy better things, and cheaper, at Frankfurt than at Venice...

ALBRECHT DÜRER to Willibald Pirckheimer, 1506

156

114

115

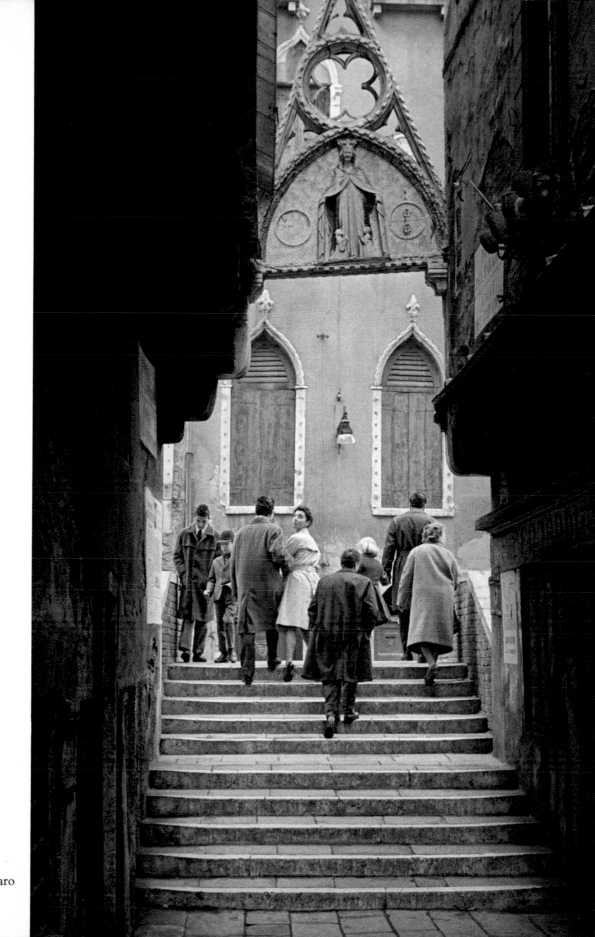

120

The silence of Venice

The silence of Venice constitutes, in my opinion, one of its greatest charms. This absence of noise is peculiarly soothing to the mind, and disposes it to contemplation. I looked out from my balcony last night, when the grand canal reflected a thousand brilliant stars on its water, turbid though it be; and the lights streaming from the windows on each side, showed like golden columns on its bosom. Gondola after gondola glided along, from some of which soft music stole on the ear, and sometimes their open windows revealed some youthful couple with their guitars, or some more matured ones, partaking their light repast of fruit and cakes; while not unfrequently a solitary male figure was seen reclined on the seat absorbed in the perusal of some book. The scene realized some of the descriptions of Venice read years ago; and except that the gondolas were small in number, and the lights from the houses few and far between, I could have fancied that no change had occurred since the descriptions I referred to were written. The morning light reveals the melancholy alteration; and as I stood on the same balcony to-day, and saw the muddy canal with a few straggling gondolas gliding over it, the defaced and mutilated palaces, and the reduced population, all brought out into distinctness by the bright beams of the sun, I could hardly believe it was the same scene that looked so well last night. Moonlight is a great beautifier, and especially of all that has been touched by the finger of decay, from a palace to – a woman. It softens what is harsh, renders fairer what is fair, and disposes the mind to a tender melancholy in harmony with all around.

LADY BLESSINGTON The Idler in Italy, 1839–40

163

21 Palazzo Loredan, Rio di S. Canciano

Sixteenth-century Venice

This City of Venice is very fair, and greatly to be commended, wherein is good order for all things: and also it is very strong and populous: it standeth upon the main Sea, and hath many Islands about it, that belong to it.

To tell you of the duke of Venice, and of the Seignory: there is one chosen that ever beareth the name of a duke, but in truth he is but servant to the Seignory, for of himself he can do little: it is no otherwise with him, then with a Priest that is at Mass upon a festival day, which putting on his golden garment, seemeth to be a great man, but if any man come unto him, and crave some friendship at his hands, he will say, you must go to the Masters of the Parish, for I can not pleasure you, otherwise than by preferring of your suite: and so it is with the duke of Venice, if any man having a suite, come to him, and make his complaint, and deliver his supplication, it is not in him to help him, but he will tell him, You must come this day, or that day, and then I will prefer your suite to the Seignory, and do you the best friendship that I may. Furthermore, if any man bring a letter unto him, he may not open it, but in the presence of the Seignory, and they are to see it first, which being read, perhaps they will deliver it to him, perhaps not. Of the Seignory there be about three hundred, and about fourty of the privy Council of Venice, who usually are arrayed in gowns of crimson Satin, or crimson Damask, when they sit in Council.

In the City of Venice, no man may wear a weapon, except he be a soldier for the Seignory, or a scholar of Padua, or a gentleman of great countenance, and yet he may not do that without licence.

As for the women of Venice, they be rather monsters, than women. Every Shoemaker's or Tailor's wife will have a gown of silk, and one to carry up her train, wearing their shoes very near half a yard high from the ground: if a stranger meet one of them, he will surely think by the state that she goeth with, that he meeteth a Lady.

RICHARD HAKLUYT The Principal Navigations, Voyages,
Traffiques and Discoveries of the English Nation, 1598–1600

Melancholy decay

This Venice, which was a haughty, invincible, magnificent Republic for nearly fourteen hundred years; whose armies compelled the world's applause whenever and wherever they battled; whose navies well nigh held dominion of the seas, and whose merchant fleets whitened the remotest oceans with their sails and loaded these piers with the products of every clime, is fallen a prey to poverty, neglect, and melancholy decay. Six hundred years ago, Venice was the Autocrat of Commerce; her mart was the great commercial centre, the distributing-house from whence the enormous trade of the Orient was spread abroad over the Western world. Today her piers are deserted, her warehouses are empty, her merchant fleets are vanished, her armies and her navies are but memories. Her glory is departed, and with her crumbling grandeur of wharves and palaces about her she sits among her stagnant lagoons, forlorn and beggared, forgotten by the world. She that in her palmy days commanded the commerce of a hemisphere and made the weal or woe of nations with a beck of her puissant finger is become the humblest among the peoples of the Earth – a peddler of glass-beads for women, and trifling toys and trinkets for school-girls and children.

MARK TWAIN The Innocents Abroad, 1869

165

VENICE

White swan of cities, slumbering in thy nest
So wonderfully built among the reeds
Of the lagoon, that fences thee and feeds,
As sayeth thy old historian and thy guest!

White water-lily, cradled and caressed
By ocean streams and from the silt and weeds
Lifting thy golden filaments and seeds,
Thy sun-illumined spires, thy crown and crest!

White phantom city, whose untrodden streets
Are rivers, and whose pavements are the shifting
Shadows of palaces and strips of sky;

I wait to see thee vanish like the fleets
Seen in mirage, or towers of cloud uplifting
In air their unsubstantial masonry.

HENRY WADSWORTH LONGFELLOW

122 Chiesa della Madonna dell'Orto, Rio Brass

123

124

126

127

128

The bridges

Where an alley meets a water-way, there you have a Venetian bridge. The bridges, as Evelyn observed, 'tack the city together'. There are more to the square mile in Venice than anywhere else on earth – more than 450 of them, ranging from the gigantic twin spans of the causeway to the dainty little private bridge on Giudecca which, if you open its wicket gate and cross its planks, deposits you prudently in the garden of the Queen of Greece. There is the Bridge of Fists and the Bridge of Straw and the Bridge of the Honest Woman and the Bridge of Courtesy and the Bridge of Humility and the Little Bridge and the Long Bridge and the Bridge of Paradise and the Bridge of Sighs, where Byron stood, lost in sentimental but misinformed reverie.

The arched bridge turned the canals into highways; but to this day many of the Venetian bridges are so low, so dark and so narrow that the gondolier has to crouch low on his poop to get through them, while his passengers clutch their new straw hats and laugh at their own echoes (and if it is one of those bridges whose undersides are flecked with moving water-reflections, going beneath it is like gliding behind a silent waterfall). The ubiquity of bridges has given the Venetians their peculiar clipped gait, and contributes heavily to the swollen ankles and unsteady heels with which unaccustomed visitors, swearing inexpressible enjoyment, stagger back to a restorative bath after an afternoon of sightseeing.

JAMES MORRIS Venice, 1960

173

32 Palazzo Widmann-Foscari, Rio di S. Canescino

An epitome

Having now so amply declared unto thee most of the principall things of this thrise-renowned and illustrious citie, I will briefly by way of an Epitome mention most of the other particulars thereof, and so finally shut up this narration: There are reported to be in Venice and the circumjacent islands (which are in number twenty five) two hundred Churches in which are one hundred forty three paire of Organs, fifty foure Monasteries, twenty sixe Nunneries, fifty sixe Tribunals or places of judgement, seventeene Hospitals, sixe Companies or Fraternities, whereof I have before spoken; one hundred sixty five marble statues of worthy personages, partly equestriall, partly pedestriall, which are erected in sundry places of the cities, to the honour of those that eyther at home have prudently administred the Commonweale, or abroad valiantly fought for the same. Likewise of brasse there are twenty three, whereof one is that of Bartholomew Coleon before mentioned. Also there are twentie seven publique clocks, ten brasen gates, a hundred and fourteene Towers for bels to hang in, ten brasen horses, one hundred fifty five wells for the common use of the citizens, one hundred eighty five most delectable gardens, ten thousand Gondolaes, foure hundred and fifty bridges partly stony, partly timber, one hundred and twenty Palaces, where-of one hundred are very worthy of that name, one hundred seventy foure courts: and the totall number of soules living in the citie and about the same is thought to be about five hundred thousand, something more or lesse. For sometimes there is a catalogue made of all the persons in the citie of what sexe or age soever they be; as we may reade there was heretofore in Rome in the time of Augustus Cæsar: and at the last view there were found in the whole City as many as I have before spoken.

THOMAS CORYATE Coryat's Crudities, 1611

Venice in the eighteenth century

Venice consists of 150 islands; each of these islands contains a large number of streets: thus, in the island or quarter of Biri, formed by three canals and the sea, I counted 56 streets. The Grand Canal cuts it in two. It is divided into six quarters, which contain 72 parishes, 25 churches belonging to monks, 36 to nuns, without counting several hospitals, oratories, schools. On these islands there are 500 bridges, nearly all of stone. On the Rialto Bridge, which has a single arch, there are 48 shops and 3 passageways. Its circumference, including the Zecca and San Giorgo, is 7 miles round; that of the Arsenal alone is 2 miles.

Venice is large, and yet there is no coach-house, no stable, no court-yard, and hardly any gardens.

It is said that there are 20,000 souls at Murano. I can say nothing as to the number in Venice. All I can say is that the other quarters are probably as populated as those around St Mark's Square. I have heard it stated that there are 160,000 souls in Murano and Venice.

BARON DE MONTESQUIEU Voyage en Italie, 1728

On the Extinction of the Venetian Republic

Once did she hold the gorgeous East in fee:
  And was the safeguard of the West: the worth
  Of Venice did not fall below her birth,
Venice, the eldest Child of Liberty.
She was a maiden City, bright and free;
  No guile seduced, no force could violate;
  And, when she took unto herself a mate,
She must espouse the everlasting Sea.
And what if she had seen those glories fade,
  Those titles vanish, and that strength decay;
Yet shall some tribute of regret be paid
  When her long life hath reach'd its final day:
Men are we and must grieve when even the Shade
  Of that which once was great is pass'd away.

WILLIAM WORDSWORTH, 1802

176

134
Un Rio a Castello

135
Ponte dei Tre Archi

136
Ponte Cannaregio

137

137, 139

138 Via (

Rio di S. A

140 Zattere ai
Gesuati

141 Ponte dell
Calcina

142 Campo
dei Mori

143 S. Pietro
di Castello

144 La Giudecc
Calle del
Forner

145 La Giudecc

146 La Giudecc
Fondament
S. Eufemia

147 Rio S. Niccolò

148 Palazzo Ariani

NOTES TO THE PLATES

1 St Mark's Square, facing the west front of the Basilica of St Mark and the Campanile (325 ft high). Originally dating from the 9th century, this tower was rebuilt more or less as it now appears after the earthquake of 1511; it collapsed on 14 July 1902 and was re-erected 1905–12.

2 The view from the Clock Tower (plate 35) across the Piazzetta with its twin columns surmounted by the winged lion of St Mark and by St Theodore with his crocodile, towards the island of San Giorgio. On the left can be seen the façade of St Mark's and, beyond, part of the Doge's Palace (above which the campanile of the church of San Giorgio Maggiore is visible). On the right, beyond the Loggetta of the Campanile, stretches the façade of the Old Library.

3 St Mark's Square, looking west. It is bounded on two sides by what were once the residences of the city's 'procurators': on the north side, the Procuratie Vecchie (1480–1517), on the south, the Procuratie Nuove (begun 1584 by Scamozzi and finished 1640 by Longhena); at the far end, the Ala Nuovissima (Ala Napoleonica) or Fabbrica Nuova, built 1810 by Giuseppe Soli on the orders of Napoleon on the site of the church of San Geminiano.

4 View from the tower of the church of San Giorgio Maggiore. From left to right: the Giardinetto San Marco laid out between the south side of the Procuratie Nuove and the waterfront on the instructions of Napoleon; the three-storeyed Zecca, built 1535 by Sansovino as the Mint and now the Marcian Library; the Old Library, backed by the Campanile San Marco; the Piazzetta with its two columns; the Doge's Palace with the domes of St Mark's beyond; the Ponte della Paglia and, abutting the Palace, the Prigioni built 1560–1614, formerly the State prisons and now occupied by the Circolo Artistico.

5 The Piazzetta di San Marco in the rain.

6–16 The BASILICA OF ST MARK, the cathedral of Venice since 1807, was erected to house the bones of the city's patron saint, which were brought from Alexandria in 829; its present appearance dates from the 11th century.

6 The 'Prima Arcata', known as the Porch of Sant'Alipio, is the northernmost of the five porches of the west front. Within the tympanum formed by the Moorish

arch the symbols of the Evangelists are shown in relief. The mosaic in the vaulting above, the façade's only mosaic to be preserved from among the original ones of 1260-70, represents the deposition of the relics of St Mark in the Basilica, and shows the church as it then was.

7 The west front with its decorative features dating from the Byzantine era to the 19th century constitutes a veritable museum of sculptures and mosaics. The mosaic above the central porch was executed 1836-38 by Salandri after a cartoon of L. Querena's, replacing a 13th-century mosaic.

8 The porphyry group of four emperors adorning the south façade represents the four tetrarchs of Diocletian. This Egyptian sculpture of the 4th century was in the first place probably intended as a support for an entablature. Popular tradition has it that these are the four 'blackmoors' who tried to steal the treasure of St Mark's.

9 Occupying a prominent position in the centre of the west front are the four bronze horses which, when Constantinople was sacked during the Fourth Crusade of 1204, the Doge Enrico Dandolo had removed from the tower of the Hippodrome and brought to Venice. The horses had come to Constantinople from the island of Chios; some authorities regard them as Greek work of the 4th-3rd centuries BC, others as Roman.

10 Detail from the extreme left of the west front: set between two pillars on the lower pediment, the statue of an old man with a water-jar, thought to derive from the older façade; within the upper arch, a Byzantine relief with two pigeons; on the right, a relief showing Hercules with the boar of Erymanthos, thought to be a Roman copy of a Greek original.

11 Detail from the bronze door of the central porch; Byzantine work of the 6th century.

12 Mosaics in the atrium (plate 14), third dome with scenes from the story of Joseph: Joseph is cast into the pit by his brothers; the brothers parley at table with merchants who have come by camel, over the sale of Joseph.

13 Detail from the story of Jesus on one of four alabaster columns carrying the canopy of the High Altar. The provenance of these reliefs, which recall Early Christian representations of a beardless Christ, is uncertain; some consider them to be Syrian or Egyptian work of the 5th-6th centuries, others attribute them to 13th-century Venice.

14 The portico (atrium) with its 13th-century mosaics, looking south.

15 View from the main entrance down the nave towards the High Altar. The figures on the marble screen date from 1394; the altar itself is Gothic. The mosaics (12th-13th centuries) in the dome above the altar depict Christ's gospel as foretold by the Prophets. In the apse, Christ enthroned, after a design by Pietro Mosaicista, 1506.

16 Mosaic of an angel, dating from the 12th century, on a pendentive of the dome above the vestibule.

17-30 THE DOGE'S PALACE: In the 9th century the seat of government was removed from the Rialto to this location. In 1116 the Emperor Henry V was received here eleven years after the building had been re-erected following a fire; Doge Sebastiano Ziani had the Palace restored for the famous meeting in 1177 between Frederick Barbarossa and Pope Alexander III, which he initiated. The building was enlarged during the 13th and 14th centuries, notably in 1340 following the formation of the Great Council, and so gradually acquired its present form; the façade fronting the Piazzetta dates from the 15th century.

17 In 1438 Giovanni Buon and his son Bartolomeo started work on the ornamental portal known as the Porta della Carta, which was finished five years later. The marble group above the entrance shows Doge Francesco Foscari kneeling in front of the Lion of St Mark; the original was destroyed in 1797 and replaced by a copy. Set into the north corner of the west front (right) is a Renaissance carving of the Judgment of Solomon, a work of the Tuscan school of sculpture; on the corner-pillar of the upper arcade, the Angel of Peace.

18 The south-west corner, with its marble sculpture of Adam and Eve and the serpent; on the corner-pillar of the upper arcade, the Archangel Michael. Both date from the end of the 14th century.

19 The balcony in the centre of the south front is crowned by a statue of Venezia as Justice, by Alessandro Vittoria, 1579.

20 The best view of the building is to be obtained from the water.

21 Set amid the tracery of quatrefoils decorating the west façade is a medallion by a 'Gothic' Lombard sculptor that depicts Venezia as Justice enthroned.

22-24 From the wealth of carved figures on the capitals of the portico columns: on the south façade the fifth capital from the right. The heads of five emperors of Antiquity appear between elaborate foliage (22). The central one is Titus Vespasian. In representing the Virtues and Sins on the capitals of the south façade the 15th-century sculptors have used their Venetian contemporaries as models (23, 24).

25-26 The marble group on the south-east corner, attributed to a Lombard sculptor of about 1500, depicts Noah drunk: on the south side, Noah; on the east side, Shem and Tapheth seek to conceal his nakednes.

27 On the east side of the Foscari arch opposite the Scala dei Giganti, statues of Adam and Eve carved by Antonio Rizzo in 1476 are set in two niches. The marble originals are now inside the Palace, having been replaced here by bronze copies.

28 The courtyard with the clock tower; right, the Foscari arch with the domes of St Mark's beyond.

29 Following the conflagration of 1574, the Senate Chamber (Sala dei Pregadi) was rebuilt by the 'Proto' (architect in chief) of the time, Antonio da Ponte. In the centre of the richly embellished ceiling, executed in 1581 by Cristoforo Sorte of Verona, is a representation of Venezia triumphant designed by Tintoretto.

30 The chamber of the Great Council (Maggior Consiglio) was restored after its destruction by fire in 1577. This great hall, 177 ft long and 82 ft wide, has a ceiling

by Sorte with inset paintings by leading artists of the day, the whole of the back wall (23 ft × 72 ft) being covered with a representation of Paradise by Tintoretto.

31 The bronze pedestals of the three tall flagpoles on the Piazza in front of St Mark's are decorated with allegorical scenes by Alessandro Leopardi (1505).

32 Among the many representations of the Lion of St Mark the one Antonio Gai made for the bronze door of the Loggetta (plate 37) is among the most attractive.

33 In countless squares and courtyards are to be found the 'vere da pozzo' or well-heads, two of the most elaborate ones, in bronze, being in the courtyard of the Doge's Palace. Our plate shows the more southerly of the two, which Niccolò dei Conti fashioned in 1556; the central garland frames a head of Doge Francesco Venier.

34 The Stairway of the Giants (Scala dei Giganti) – named after the two huge figures of Mercury and Neptune (1566) by Sansovino set up on either side – was built 1484–1501 to the designs of Antonio Rizzi as a ceremonial approach to the State apartments from the courtyard.

35 The Clock Tower in the north-east corner of St Mark's Square was built 1496–1499 to the designs of Moro Coducci; the side-structures, which received an additional storey in 1755, were added 1500–06. The clock is the work of an artificer named Ramiere and his son, from Reggio.

36 One of the two 'Moors' on the platform of the Clock Tower, who strike the hours; these great bronze figures were made by Ambrosio de la Anchore in 1494.

37 The Loggetta at the foot of the Campanile as seen from the southern end of the west front of St Mark's. Designed by Sansovino, it was built 1537–49.

38 In the Piazzetta.

39 Work on the Old Library (Libreria Vecchia di San Marco) was begun in 1536 to the designs of Sansovino. After numerous interruptions – one of which was due to the collapse of some vaulting, which resulted in the architect being flung into prison – the building was completed fifty-two years later, by which time Sansovino had died. It was meant to house in particular the rare collection of Codices which Cardinal Bessarione had donated to the Republic in 1468.

40 The Molo, the waterside extension of the Piazzetta, with the Doge's Palace.

41 The famous Bridge of Sighs (Ponte dei Sospiri) connects the east side of the Doge's Palace (left) with the old State prisons (right), crossing the Rio di Palazzo.

42 The church of San Giorgio Maggiore with its nearly 200 ft-high campanile, as seen from the Molo.

43 The interior of San Giorgio Maggiore. Palladio began work on the church in 1566, but it was not finished until 1580 after the famous architect's death.

44 The Ponte della Veneta Marina of 1877 spans the Rio della Tana.

45 View of the Riva degli Schiavoni from the tower of San Giorgio Maggiore: left, the neo-classic façade of the church of Santa Maria della Pietà or della Visitazione; right, towards the rear, the tall campanile of the church of San Francesco della Vigna.

46 Looking across the Fondamenta San Biagio towards the Dogana di Mare and the church of Santa Maria della Salute.

47 On the Riva degli Schiavoni stands the 15th-century Palazzo Dandolo; it subsequently belonged in succession to the Gritti, Bernardo and Mocenigo families, finally becoming the Hotel Danieli, renowned as a hostelry since the 19th century. In the foreground, the Ponte del Vin.

48 The façade of the church of San Moisè. Erected in 1668 thanks to a legacy from the patrician Vincenzo Fini to the designs of Alessandro Tremignon, with a crest of the donor above the central porch, it is a characteristic example of the style which Ruskin called 'Grotesque Baroque'.

49-83 The GRAND CANAL (CANAL GRANDE)

49 Looking east from the Accademia bridge: left, the Palazzo Franchetti, formerly Gussoni-Cavalli, built in the 15th century and much restored in 1896; on the far side of the Canal, the domes and towers of the church of Santa Maria della Salute, masterpiece of Baldassare Longhena, 1631–81.

50 A view across the Canal to the left bank (approaching from the Piazzetta) towards the restored Palazzo Salviati, the 15th-century Palazzo Barbaro with its recent extension and, right, the Renaissance façade of the Palazzo Dario attributed to the School of Pietro Lombardo, c. 1487.

51 Right bank (approaching from the Piazzetta). From right to left: Palazzo Contarini (15th century); the little Palazzetto Contarini-Fasan (c. 1475), known as 'Desdemona's House'; the Palazzi Manolesso-Ferro (15th century) and Flangini-Fini (17th century), which are now both part of the Grand Hotel; on the further side of the Rio delle Ostreghe, a corner of the Palazzo Gritti (Palace Hotel), first put up at the beginning of the 15th century.

52 Right bank: Palazzo Corner della Ca' Grande, seat of the Prefecture, built 1561 to the designs of Sansovino, State property since the beginning of the 19th century.

53 Left bank: Palazzo Balbi of 1582–90. Situated at a sharp bend of the Canal, it is visible from some way off.

54 Left bank: Palazzo Contarini dal Zaffo or Manzini, a Renaissance building dating from the end of the 15th century.

55 Left bank: Palazzo Loredan, a Gothic building of the 15th century; it later served as the Austrian Embassy and became known as 'Palazzo dell'Ambasciatore'.

56 Left bank: Palazzo Rezzonico, now a Museum of the Venetian 18th century, was built in the middle of the 17th century by Longhena for the Priuli-Bon family; 1745 Giorgio Massari enlarged it for the Rezzonico family by adding the top storey. Robert Browning died here in 1889.

57 View from the Ponte Foscari down the Rio di Ca' Foscari to the Grand Canal; facing, from right to left: Palazzo Erizzo, later Nani Mocenigo (15th century); Palazzo Contarini 'delle Figure' (Early 16th century); the Case del Mocenigo, a group of buildings of the 16th–17th centuries where, among others, Giordano Bruno and Lord Byron lived.

58　Left bank: left, the 15th-century Gothic twin Palazzo Giustinian occupied 1858–59 by Wagner while composing the second Act of the opera 'Tristan and Isolde'; right, the Palazzo Foscari dating from the same period, where Doge Francesco Foscari died 1457 after he had been deposed and where Henry III of France was a guest in 1572. Today it serves as an Institute of the University.

59　Left bank: left to right, Palazzo Tiepolo, a 16th-century Renaissance building; the 15th-century Gothic Palazzo Pisani-Moretta, enlarged in the 16th century; Palazzo Barbarigo della Terrazza with its terrace (c. 1568–69).

60　Right bank: from right to left, Palazzo d'Anna-Viaro-Martinengo, later Volpi (16th century); Palazzo and Palazzetto Tron (originally 15th century); Palazzo Corner Contarini 'dei Cavalli' (c. 1445); Palazzo Grimani, built in the 16th century to the designs of Michele Sammichele of Verona, now the Court of Appeal.

61　View from the Rialto Bridge, looking north.

62　Right bank: right, Palazzo Farsetti, formerly Dandolo; left, Palazzo Loredan, formerly Corner Piscopia. Both these 12th-century buildings with their Byzantine arcades have been used as municipal offices since 1868.

63　Looking across the Riva del Vin to the opposite (right) bank of the Canal from one of the approaches to the Rialto Bridge; left, the Palazzi Loredan and Farsetti.

64　On the steps of the Rialto Bridge. Up and down them the pedestrians pass in a perpetual stream, as they do across the countless other bridges large and small.

65　The Rialto Bridge, south side. As winner of a competition in which the leading architects of Italy took part, Antonio da Ponte was entrusted in 1587 with the building of a stone bridge across the Canal here in the old city centre.

66　Left bank: directly beside the Rialto Bridge stands the Palazzo dei Camerlenghi, a Renaissance building erected 1525–28 to the designs of Guglielmo dei Grigi of Bergamo.

67　Right bank: the 12th-century Fondaco dei Tedeschi, formerly the German warehouse, was redesigned in 1508 by Giorgio Spavento following a fire. The exterior was adorned with frescoes by Giorgione and possibly Titian as well, which have since weathered away.

68　Left bank: Fondaco dei Turchi. This early 13th-century palace, which was once among the most luxurious in the city, served 1621–1838 as a place of domicile for Turkish merchants. It was extensively restored in the 19th century and now houses the National History Museum.

69–72　Each morning the gay bustle of the fish, vegetable and flower market is re-enacted in the neo-Gothic open hall of the Pescheria, built in 1907.

73–75　Gondolas and gondoliers: the two commonest types of gondola are the one operated by a single boatman and used for hire, and the double-oared traghetto which is used to ferry people across the Canal at a number of strategic points.

76　Right bank: Ca' d'Oro, the most famous example of the ornate late Gothic palace style of Venice, erected c. 1421–40 by Marin Contarini around an extant 13th-century building. The embellishment is in part the work of Giovanni and Bartolomeo Buon, and was extensively restored by Matteo Raverti in the 19th century. In 1916 Baron Franchetti donated the house, which since 1927 has been open to the public, to the State.

77 Left bank: Palazzo Pesaro, a stately 17th-century building begun 1679 by Longhena and finished 1710 after his death, now makes up the Galleria d'Arte Moderna and the Museo Orientale.

78 Right bank: right, Ca' da Mosto, since the 13th century the seat of a family of famous seafarers, still retains parts of the old Byzantine structure; from the 15th to the 17th centuries it was the Albergo del Leon Bianco, a famous hostelry where, among other notabilities, the Emperor Joseph II stayed. The tower beyond the Rio dei Santi Apostoli belongs to the church of that name (17th–18th centuries). Left, the Palazzo Mangilli-Valmarana, designed about 1760 for the English ambassador and collector Joseph Smith by Antonio Visentini, the top storey being added later. The poet Rilke was among those who lived here.

79 Right bank, opposite the Pescheria: right, the Palazzo Michiel da Brusà, a Gothic building restored 1777; left, the Palazzo Michiel dalle Colonne, also called Donà dalle Rose, dating from the second half of the 17th century.

80 Right bank: Palazzo Vendramin Calergi, also known as the Palazzo Vendramin after another of its owners; a fine example of the 'Lombard' style, it was planned by Moro Coducci at the beginning of the 16th century and finished 1809 by Pietro Lombardo and his assistants. Wagner died here on 13 February 1883. The stately apartments serve as a casino now.

81 Right bank: at the point where the Cannaregio branches off from the Grand Canal stands the 18th-century Palazzo Labia; beside it, the church of Santa Geremia, restored in the 18th century; the campanile is the original 13th-century structure.

82 Left bank: visitors leaving the railway station are greeted by the slim domical structure of the church of San Simone Piccolo, built by Giovanni Scalfurotto 1718–38.

83 Right bank: on the Fondamenta degli Scalzi stands the church of Santa Maria di Nazareth degli Scalzi (the Barefooted), built in the 17th century to the designs of Longhena for the Carmelites; the Baroque façade is the work of Sardi.

84 The splendid façade of the Scuola Grande di San Rocco, newly erected in 1515 for a brotherhood founded in the 15th century, dates from 1535; it was designed by Antonio Scarpagnino. Tintoretto embellished the interior 1564–77 with a series of fifty-six paintings.

85 Facing the Campo San Rocco, at right angles to the façade of the Scuola, stands the east front of the church of San Rocco. It was redesigned 1765–71 by B. Maccaruzzi, who enlarged the original structure of 1489.

86 The apse of the church of Santa Maria Gloriosa dei Frari, called Frari for short. This church, founded by the Franciscans in the 13th century, was rebuilt from 1338 onwards as a great brick edifice of Gothic type; for centuries it served as burial place for Doges and other notables.

87 The magnificent equestrian statue in the Campo Santi Giovanni e Paolo of the Condottiere Bartolomeo Colleoni who died 1475 in the service of Venice. It was the last work (1481–88) of the sculptor Verrocchio.

88 The view across the Rio dei Mendicanti of the Scuola Grande di San Marco, one of the six 'great schools' of Venice's religious, charitable brotherhoods, founded 1260; today the Ospedale Civile, it was rebuilt by Pietro Lombardo and his assistants after the fire of 1485.

89 In 1481 Pietro Lombardo fashioned this great gateway to the Campiello of the Scuola di San Giovanni Evangelista, a brotherhood of 'Batutti' founded 1261; they had their quarters and ran a hospital here from 1340 onward.

90 The little Campo dell'Abbazia: left, the 15th-century Scuola Vecchia della Misericordia; right, the church of Santa Maria Valverde della Misericordia, a 10th-century foundation with a Baroque façade by Clemente Moli dating from 1659. The well-head in the foreground is Gothic.

91 The façade, made from various types of marble, of the little church of Santa Maria dei Miracoli, a fine example of Lombardo-Venetian Renaissance work by Pietro Lombardo and his School, 1481–86.

92 The church of San Zaccaria, founded in the 9th century; the present building was constructed 1444–65 by Antonio Gambello, the Renaissance façade added 1480–1500 by Moro Coducci.

93 Work on Santi Giovanni e Paolo or San Zanipolo, the great Gothic church of the Dominicans, which with the Frari church houses the most notable tombs of the Republic, was begun in the 13th century and was consecrated in 1430.

94 Rio dei Greci with the 15th-century; Gothic Palazzo Zorzi; beyond is the campanile, erected 1587–92 by Bernardo Ongarin to Sorella's design, of the church of San Giorgio dei Greci, assigned to the Orthodox Greeks.

95 In La Fenice theatre during a gala performance. Built 1790–92 by Antonio Selva and restored by Meduna after the fire of 1836, this is one of the most attractive tiered theatres in the world. It has been the scene of many noteworthy opera premières.

96 Rio di Palazzo.

97 A secluded canal.

98 The Corte del Milion, the square named after Marco Polo's famous record of his travels, still retains some of that 13th-century character it possessed when the Venetian ventured to the Far East. House No. 5858 seen in the photograph is known as the Casa di Marco Polo.

99 View of the Rio dei Miracoli from the Ponte Marco Polo: left, the block containing the Teatro Malibran, where Marco Polo had a house.

100 La Fenice bridge and canal.

101 Fondamenta dell'Osmarin by the Rio of the same name, on the opposite side of which can be seen the Palazzo Priuli.

102 Campo San Provolo.

103 Palazzo Contarini in the San Luca quarter: the five-storeyed spiral stairway 'Scala del Bovolo' facing the courtyard was built 1499 by Giovanni Candi and restored in the 17th century.

104 Looking from the Ponte Commeda across the Rio di Sant'Antonia towards the Scuola di San Giorgio degli Schiavoni, built in the 16th century by the Dalmatian Brotherhood (Schiavoni = Slavs); the chapel's façade is the work of Giovanni de Zan.

105 Looking up the Ghetto Nuovo canal from the Fondamenta di Ghetto Nuovissimo; the wooden bridge leads to the Campo di Ghetto Nuovo.

106 A characteristic alley (Calle).

107 Campo di Ghetto Nuovo. The term 'Ghetto' to denote a quarter allotted to the Jewish inhabitants was first applied here in Venice.

108 Campo Santa Margherita became one of the city's largest squares in the 19th century, when several canals were filled in. On the far side stands the truncated tower of the former church of Santa Margherita.

109 Campo Santo Stefano or Francesco Morosini, with the church of Santo Stefano on the right. The statue is a memorial to the philologist Niccolò Tommaseo (1882).

110 Campo San Polo (Paolo): right, the 18th-century Palazzo Tiepolo-Maffetti.

111 Campo Morosini. In the squares of Venice there is no motorized traffic to interrupt the children at play.

112 View of Campo San Tomà from the church of that name. Closing the square at its western end is the façade of the Scuola dei Calegheri (Cobblers' Guild) dating from 1478, behind which towers the campanile of the Frari church.

113 Wharf on the Rio dei Mendicanti.

114 Looking up the Rio San Polo from the Ponte San Polo, with the Palazzo Michiel Olivo (15–16th centuries) on the left.

115 Rio di Palazzo Pesaro.

116 The narrow Calle del Paradiso, where it emerges on to the Ponte del Paradiso, is spanned by a Gothic arch depicting the Madonna della Misericordia and the coat of arms of the Foscari and Mocenigo families.

117 Fondamenta San Tomà: beyond the bridge of the same name is to be seen the Palazzo Centani, formerly Rizzi (15th century), better known as the Casa di Goldoni, where the playwright was born 1707 and which since 1952 has housed the Institute for Theatrical Studies.

118 In the Calle Terrà dei Nomboli beside Goldoni's house.

119 Courtyard of Goldoni's house (Palazzo Centani) with Gothic well-head and open stairway.

120 In the middle of the busy Campo San Bartolomeo, near the Rialto bridge, stands the bronze statue of the playwright Carlo Goldoni, erected in 1883. The statue is the work of Antonio dal Zotto, the pedestal is by Pellegrino Orefice.

121 Palazzo Loredan-Grifalconi (16th century) beside the Rio di San Canciano.

122 The façade of the church of the Madonna dell'Orto or St Christopher (Gothic, 15th–16th centuries) seen from across the Rio Brasso.

123 San Francesco della Vigna, designed by Sansovino; the monumental façade was added 1568–72 by Andrea Palladio.

124 The former church of Santa Giustina, built by Longhena in the 17th century, where the G.B. Benedetti Liceo Scientifico is now located.

125 Gothic well-head in the Campo San Marziale.

126 Sculptured head above a gateway on the Fondamenta del Dose, opposite the Ponte del Paradiso.

127 Wall decoration on the tower of the former church of Santa Margherita.

128 Facing the Ponte Forner in the Santo Stae quarter is the Gothic portal (13th century) of the Palazzo Agnusdio with its early 15th-century ornamental carving.

129 The cloisters of Santo Stefano, built 1532 and extended in the 17th century. The former convent buildings now house the revenue office.

130 Rio di Ca' Garzoni with the Palazzo Pisani-Moretta (plate 59) on the far side of the Grand Canal.

131 Rio dei Greci.

132 Rio di San Canciano, Ponte Widmann and Palazzo Widmann-Foscari, formerly Saviotti, built by Longhena and housing the art collection of the Widmann family of merchants.

133 A secluded canal-side 'street'.

134 Canal in the Castello quarter, known as Riello.

135 Ponte dei Tre Archi spanning the Cannaregio canal, built 1688 by Andrea Tirali and restored 1794.

136 Ponte di Cannaregio or Ponte delle Guglie, built 1580 and restored 1776, which spans the Cannaregio canal at its busier end near the Grand Canal.

137 Rio dell'Arsenale and the entrance to the Arsenal, which Dante described as being well worth a visit and which has been subject to several alterations since medieval times. Here the Naval Museum (Museo Storico Navale) is housed. The two towers are among the structures erected by Vittorio Gambello in the 15th century; the ornate gateway (see plate 139) was fashioned by Antonio Gambello in 1460.

138 The end of the Rio di Sant'Anna with the Via Garibaldi beyond. This, one of the island-city's few broad roadways, was constructed in 1807 by filling in the canal.

139 One of the two fine Greek lions, made of marble, now flanking the entrance to the Arsenal, which Doge Francesco Morosoni had transported from Athens in 1687; it was found beside the road that leads from Athens to Eleusis.

140 Zattere ai Gesuati, a section of the quay-side by the Canale della Giudecca: right, the Baroque façade (1668) of the Dominican church of Santa Maria del Rosario, known as Gesuati; to the left of it, the church of San Gerolamo dei Gesuati or Santa Maria della Visitazione or degli Orfani (15th–16th centuries), once part of a monastery.

141 Ponte della Calcina on the Fondamenta delle Zattere: right, the Pension Calcina, once occupied by Ruskin; next to it, the house of the Venetian scholar Apostolo Zeno (1668–1750).

142 Campo dei Mori, where the Arabs once had their trading establishment: right the Palazzo Mastelli with 13th-century effigies of the 'Mori'. Popular tradition has it that the corner-figure represents Sior Antonio Rioba, called Pasquino, author of the first 'Pasquilli' (lampoons).

143 View across the Canale di San Pietro from the Ponte di Quintavalle: St Peter's Island with the church of San Pietro di Castello, until 1807 the cathedral of Venice; the campanile dates from 1482–88.

144 On the island of La Giudecca: Calle del Forner, Corte Grande.

145 View of the island of La Giudecca from the tower of San Giorgio Maggiore: in the left foreground, the dome of Santa Maria della Presentazione, called delle Zitelle; beyond, Il Redentore, a notable work of church architecture (1577–92) by Andrea Palladio.

146 On the island of La Giudecca: Fondamenta Sant'Eufemia.

147 Rio di San Niccolò with the 12th-century tower of the church of San Niccolò dei Mendicoli, one of the oldest in the city.

148 Palazzo Cigogna or Ariani, later Menotti, beside the Rio dell'Angelo Raffaele. The façade, dating from the second half of the 14th century, presents one of the earliest examples of typically Venetian palace decoration.

ACKNOWLEDGEMENTS

Acknowledgements are due to the Estate of the late Henry James for permission to quote from *Portraits of Places* and to Messrs Faber & Faber for the use of extracts from *Venice* by James Morris.

The photograph reproduced in the first colour plate was taken by Bruno Novarese of Florence, and that of the interior of La Fenice was kindly supplied by the Theatre Management. All the other photographs are by Martin Hürlimann.

LIST OF SOURCES